Step-by-Step

Acrylic

with Lori Lohstoeter

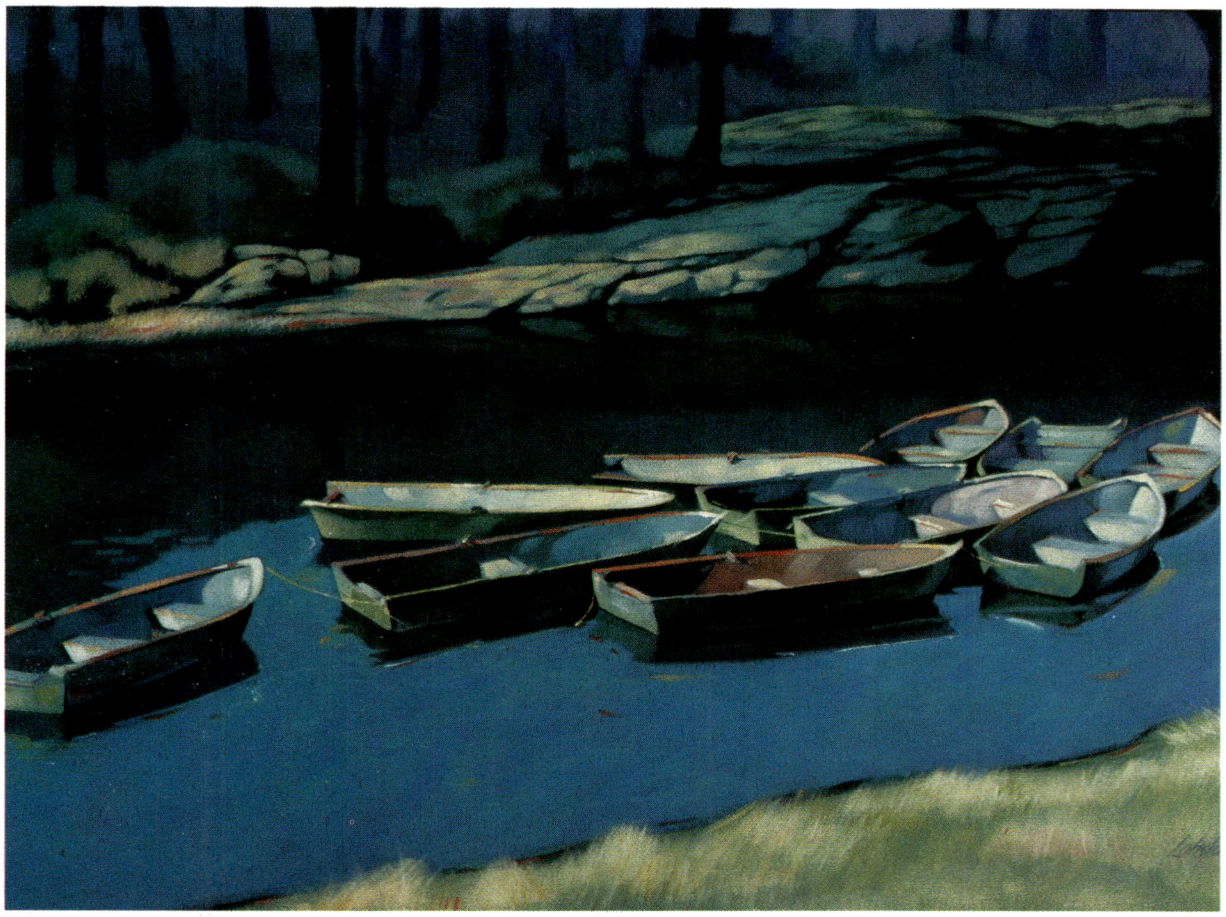

Acrylic is by far my favorite painting medium! I have logged many hours painting with other media—oils, watercolor, gouache, and pastels—but I love the vibrant colors and the variety of effects I can achieve with acrylic. I can thin the paint with water for transparent washes, much like watercolors, and build up opaque layers the way I'd use oil paints. And because of its quick drying time, acrylic allows me the freedom to paint freely and boldly; I know that within moments the surface will dry and I can paint in a completely different direction. I love this spontaneity; and, with acrylic, I can take chances that other media simply will not allow.

Once you start exploring this versatile medium, you'll find acrylic paint will allow you to express a world of creative possibilities. With the projects in this book, you'll learn a variety of techniques and tips for working in acrylic and creating special effects, for everything from landscapes and seascapes to still lifes and flowers. I'll take you step by step through each painting and hopefully provide the inspiration for you to create your own unique works of art. Acrylic is an ideal medium for experimentation, so don't be afraid to jump in there and play. I hope that you will enjoy exploring this exciting medium as much as I do!

Lori Lohstoeter

Walter Foster®

Contents

Selecting Your Supplies

I LOVE VISITING art supply stores: I'm always inspired by the colorful paints and the variety of brushes on display. Even though you'll be tempted, don't get carried away and buy one of everything! Choose a limited range, but buy the best you can afford; then expand your supplies as your skills advance. I'll share some general information about the supplies you'll need, but if you'd like to learn more, I suggest you refer to *Watercolor & Acrylic Painting Materials* by William F. Powell in Walter Foster's Artist's Library series.

Selecting Supports

Because acrylic is so versatile, you can paint on just about any surface—called a *support*—as long as it is slightly porous and isn't waxy or greasy; water-thinned acrylic colors won't adhere to oily surfaces. Most acrylic painters use canvas, a fine-surfaced fabric that is available stretched on a frame or glued to a board. If you like a smoother surface, watercolor board and primed (sealed) wood panels are good alternatives. I use canvas for very large pieces, but otherwise I prefer illustration board, a fine-grained paper mounted on a stiff board. You'll find a wide selection of supports at the art supply store. I encourage you to explore the differences among them and then choose the ones that best fit your painting style.

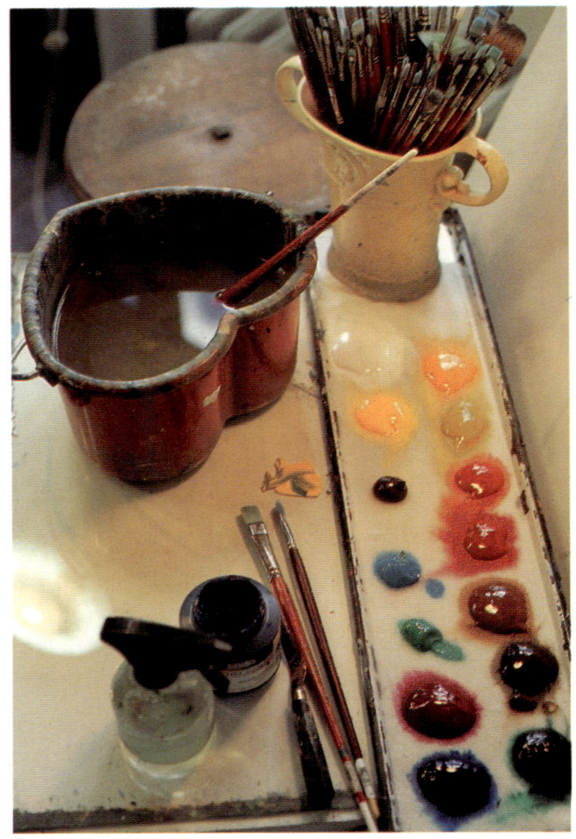

► **PREPARING YOUR PALETTE** My mixing surface is a glass-topped rolling cart. I keep my paints in an enamel tray on folded, damp paper towels, and I spritz my paints often with water to keep them from drying out and getting tacky. I always place my colors in the same place on my palette each time I paint, so I automatically know where each one is. That way I don't accidentally load the wrong color on my brush. I also place my paints in order from light to dark, grouping like colors together (reds with reds, blues with blues, and so on).

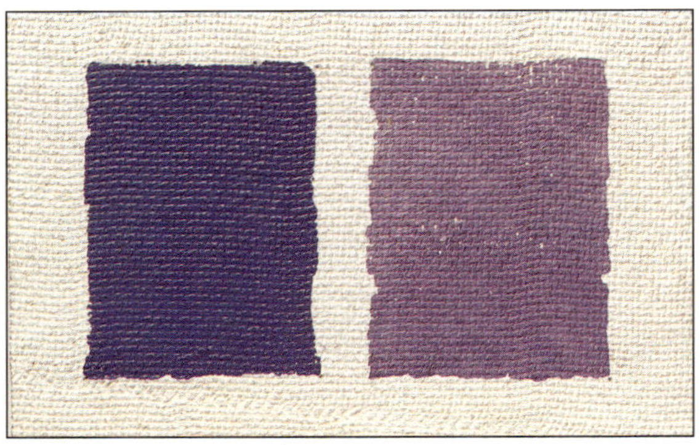

Primed pressed wood panels (rough side)

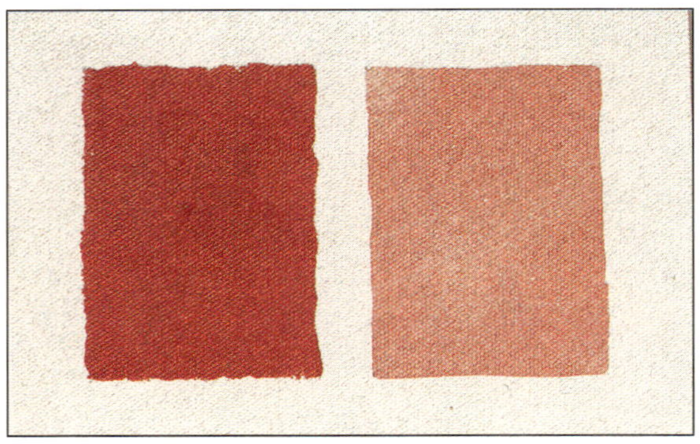

Primed pressed wood panels (smooth side)

Illustration board

Canvas board

◄ **DISTINGUISHING SUPPORTS** Some supports, such as illustration board and canvas, are paint-ready at the time of purchase. Others, like pressed wood panels, have a porous surface that needs to be primed with a sealer (usually acrylic gesso) first to make it less absorbent. Different surfaces also have different textures—smooth to rough—which affect the appearance of the paint. The examples at left show how thick (left) and thin (right) applications of acrylic paint appear on the different supports.

Purchasing Paints

Acrylic paints are available from many manufacturers and come in several forms, including tubes, jars, and cans. I buy my paints in large jars, but you can choose whatever is most convenient for you. No matter what kind you decide to purchase, I do recommend investing in high-quality paints (also called "artist's quality"), as they will always make beautiful, true, mixes. The less-expensive brands (often called "student grade") use more filler, so the colors aren't as brilliant. Start with the beginning palette listed below, and then add more colors as you can afford them. Once you're familiar with your paints, you can save a little by buying only small tubes of the colors you use less frequently.

► **CHOOSING YOUR COLORS** These are the 14 colors, including white, that I use in my paintings. They make a good palette for beginners—from them you can mix just about any color you like—and they're available in most brands. Although you can also buy black paint, I prefer to create my own using a mix of phthalocyanine (abbreviated *phthalo*) green, phthalo blue, acra violet, and burnt sienna. This makes a rich black that I feel has more "life" than the premixed blacks available.

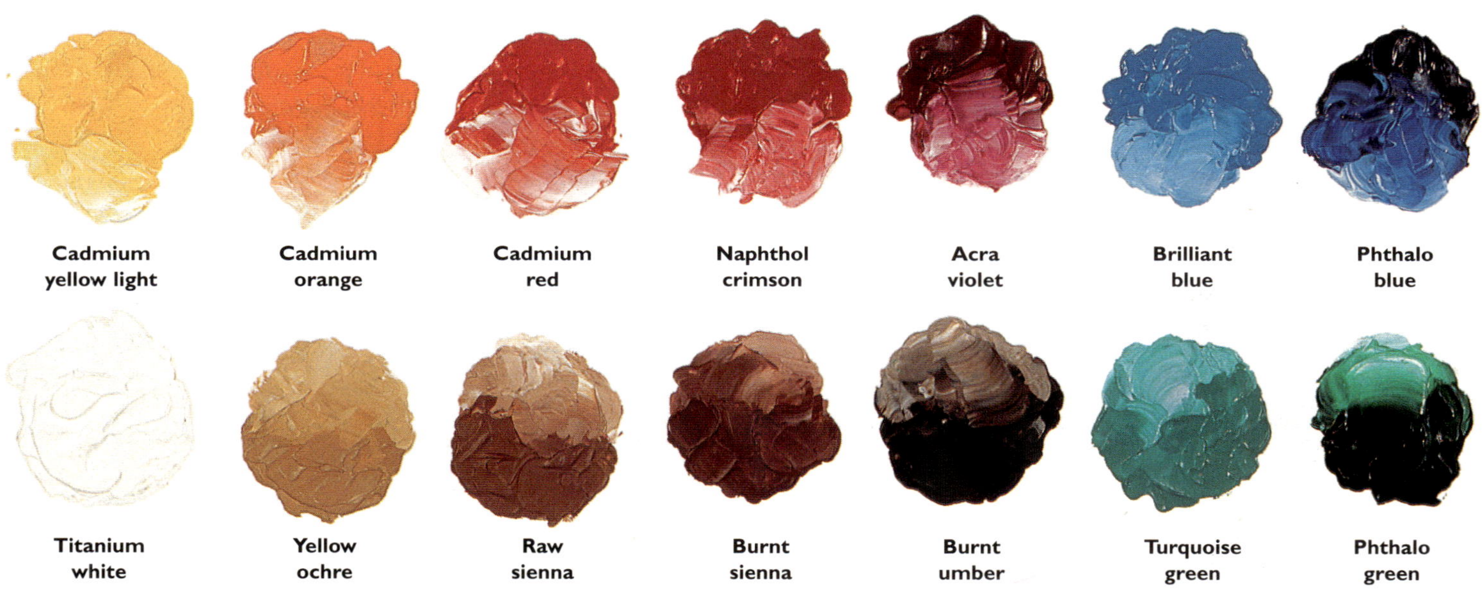

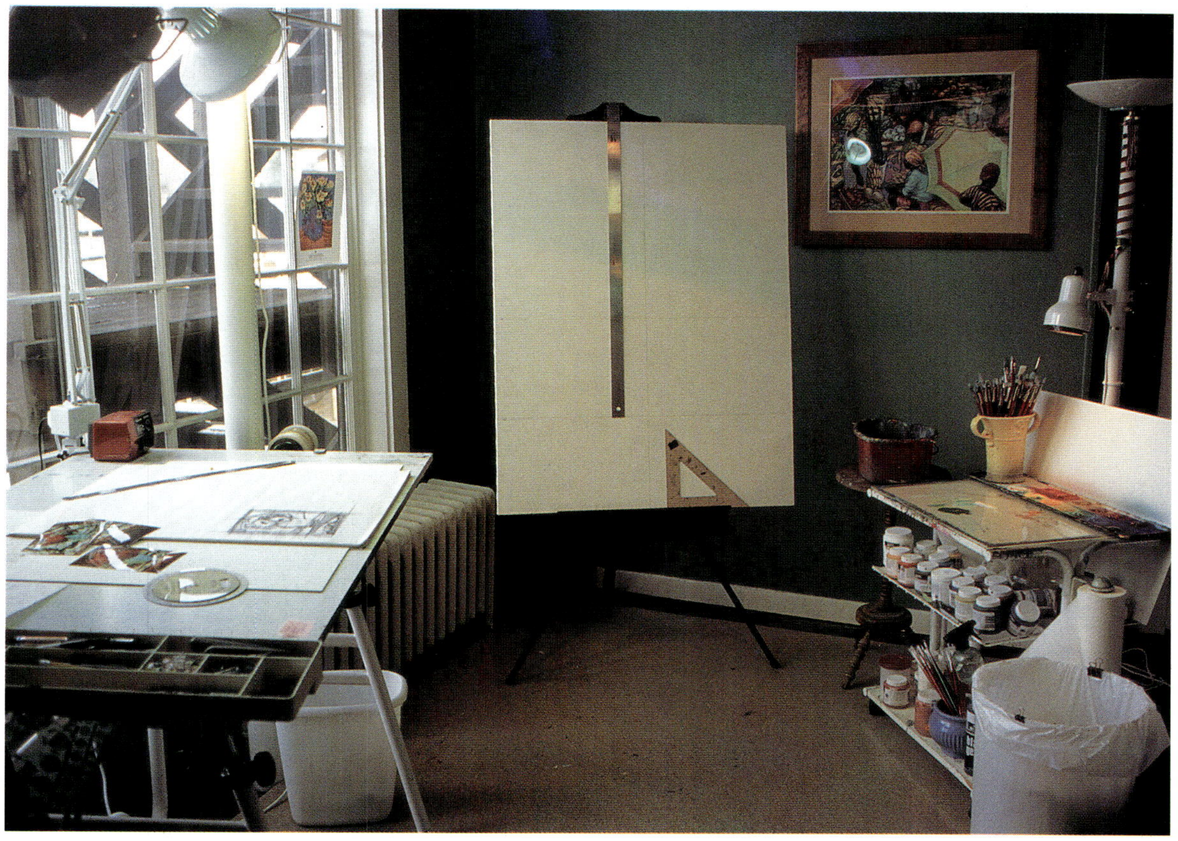

◄ **SETTING UP YOUR STUDIO** An effective studio can be very basic, as long as it's well-lit and comfortable! I use three lights to help eliminate shadows, but I rely heavily on the natural light of my large window. Whenever possible, try to use natural light. I also like to work at an angle; if you don't have a tilted drafting table like mine, you can prop your board up with some books. Just be sure to include a supportive chair in your workplace design; it will make the painting experience more pleasant—and allow you to keep at it longer!

Buying Brushes

There are many kinds of acrylic paintbrushes to choose from, categorized by hair (natural or synthetic), style (round, flat, bright, filbert, fan), and size (measured in inches and fractions of inches or by number, No. 1 being small). I prefer synthetic nylon brushes because of the way the paint glides easily off the brush. (Acrylic tends to cling to natural hair paintbrushes, and if the paint is left to dry, it can ruin a brush.) I use a combination of hog hair and synthetic brushes for my work, but you might want to experiment to see which types and sizes best suit your painting style. As with other supplies, start with just a few good-quality paintbrushes, then buy more as your skills develop.

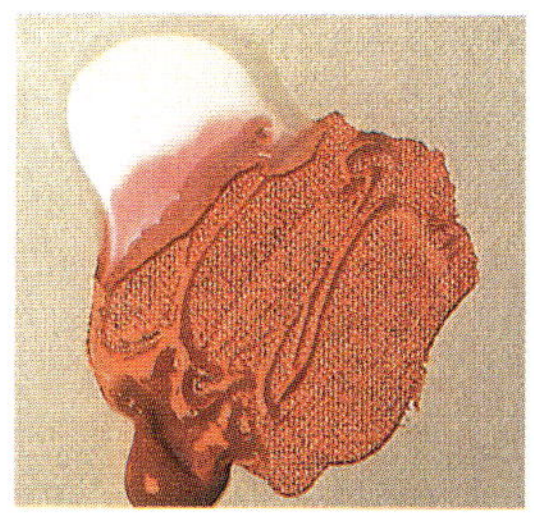

Gloss medium

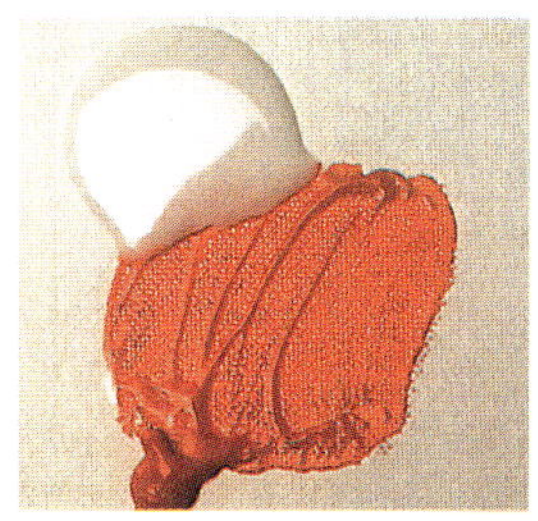

Matte medium

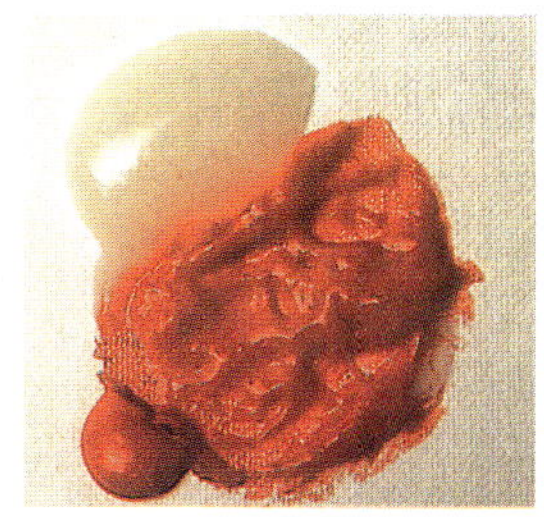

Gel medium

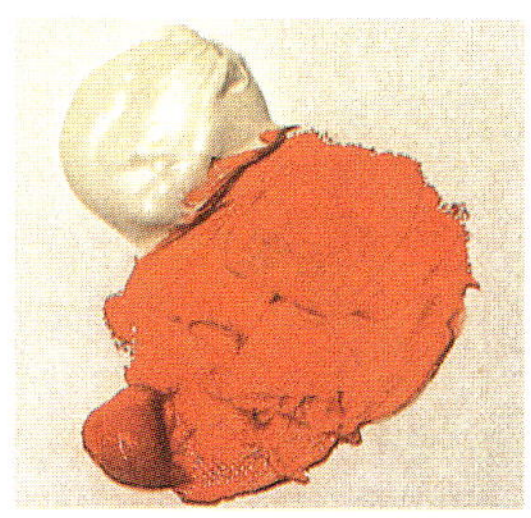

Texture medium

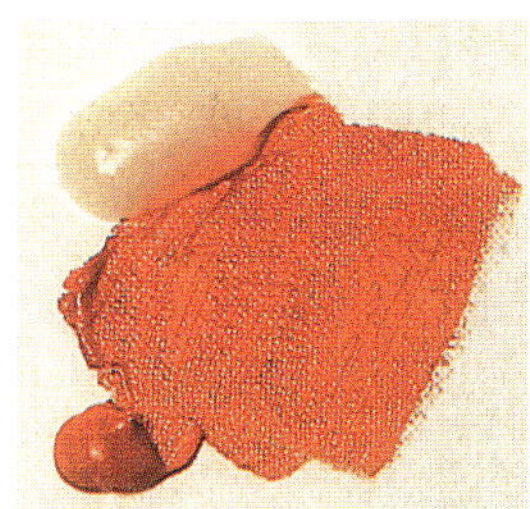

Retarding medium

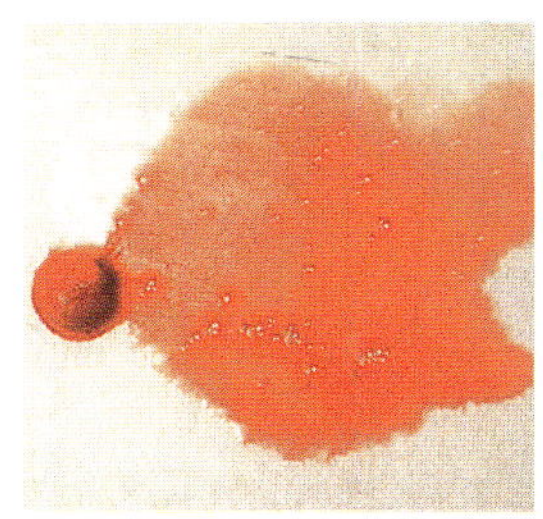

Flow improver

▲ **WORKING WITH MEDIUMS** Adding a medium to your paint changes its characteristics. Glosses thin the paint and give it a shiny surface when dry; matte mediums dry dull. Gel medium allows you to create some texture, as it thickens the paint. Texture mediums also thicken; they're used to create sharp ridges and patterns. Retarders slow the paint's drying time, and flow improvers do just that: help the paint flow easily.

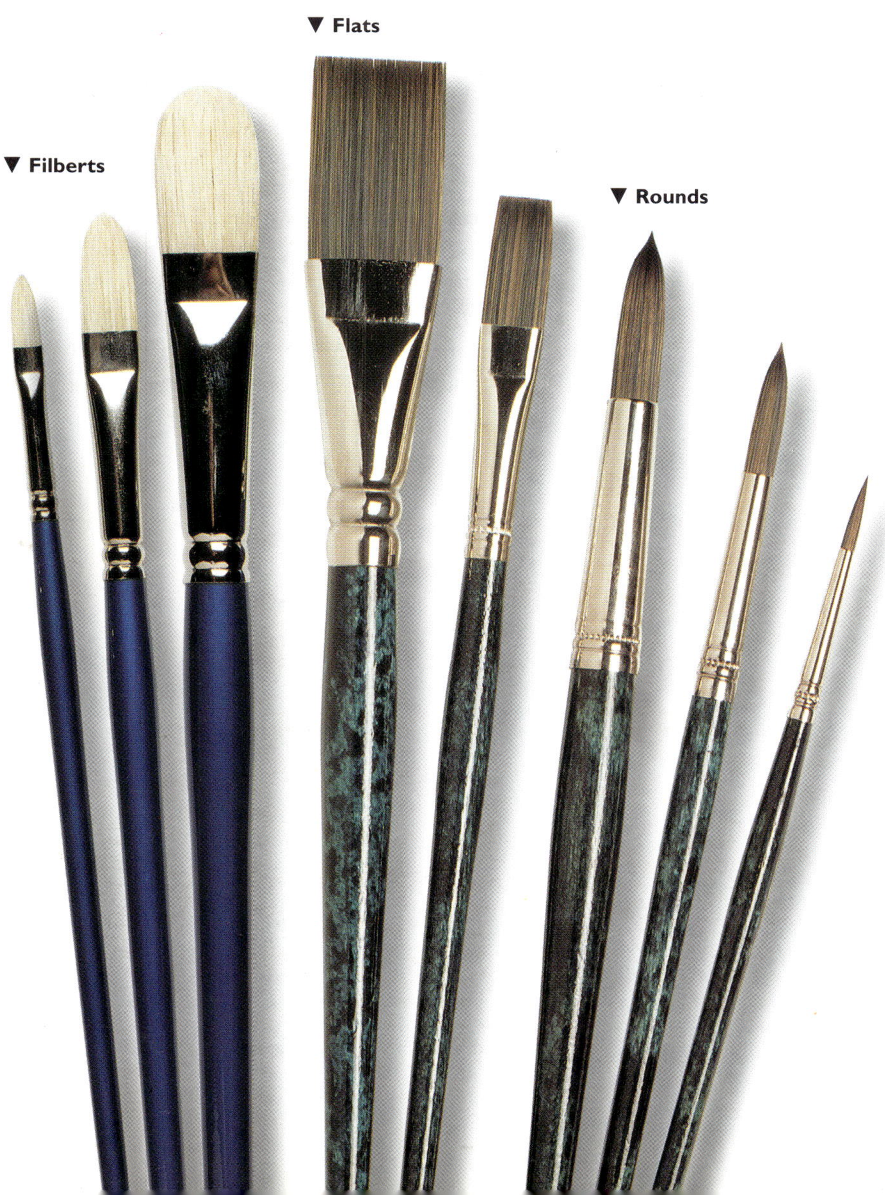

◄ **SELECTING YOUR BRUSHES** Each brush has its own function, so it's good to keep a variety on hand. Large, flat-edged brushes are ideal for washes (see page 5) and large areas of color, and smaller ones are good for detail work and refining sharp edges. I use filberts to quickly sketch outlines and silhouettes, but I do most of my work with round brushes, using the smallest sizes for the most intricate details. The rough bristles of hog hair brushes are ideal for drybrush painting (see page 19), and I love to use them to scrub in grainy sands and rock textures.

Using Painting Mediums

Because acrylic is water based, you can thin it simply by adding water, and that's all you'll need to do when you're first starting out. Once you've acquired a little more expertise, though, you might want to try mixing the colors with various painting mediums—additives that change the nature of the paint in various ways, such as making it dry slower, appear more transparent, or become thicker. Some also add luster, making the colors look more translucent than with water alone. The samples above show a few of the most popular painting mediums and how they mix with acrylic paints. Don't be alarmed by the look of the mediums; they start out with a milky white color but they become transparent when dry!

Getting to Know the Paint

YOU'VE HEARD THAT "practice makes perfect," and painting with acrylic is no exception to this rule. In this case, "practice" means getting comfortable with your paints and tools. I suggest you use a bit of inexpensive watercolor paper to start dabbling with the paints to see what effects acrylic can produce. Have fun, be playful and creative, and soon you'll come to your own conclusions about colors, consistencies, drying times, and even textures. And your ever-expanding knowledge base will contribute to fabulous future paintings!

Exploring Techniques

Acrylic is an exciting medium to explore. I use it straight from the tube or diluted with water to produce an array of different effects, from thick impasto applications to transparent washes. And I can layer the paints and combine all these techniques to create paintings full of depth, contrast, and color diversity. The samples on this page show just a few of the many exciting effects you can achieve by varying brushstroke, color, and technique. Acrylic is such a flexible medium that the possibilities are endless!

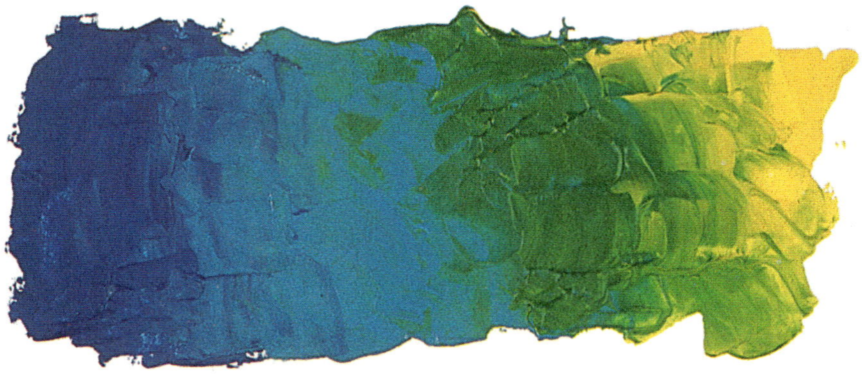

PAINTING KNIFE Knives are frequently used to mix paint, but using your knife to paint with as well as mix can add real drama to your painting. Use the flat blade to spread a thick layer of paint over the surface. Each knife stroke leaves behind thick ridges and lines where it ends, mimicking rough, complex textures like stone walls or rocky landscapes. Or you can use the edge of the blade, working quickly to create thin linear ridges that suggest and define shapes. Even the point of the knife is useful; it can scrape away paint to reveal whatever lies beneath.

▶ **BRUSHWORK** Think of brushstrokes as fingerprints: No two are exactly alike. A round brush will leave behind a different print than a flat one will, and the size of the brush will affect its imprint. Even the way you hold a brush—from the angle to the pressure and grip—will change the appearance of your strokes. You can create thin lines with the edge of any size brush, make bold strokes by applying more pressure, and taper your strokes by pressing less firmly and lifting up at the end. Try practicing the techniques shown here to get comfortable with the different strokes you can produce.

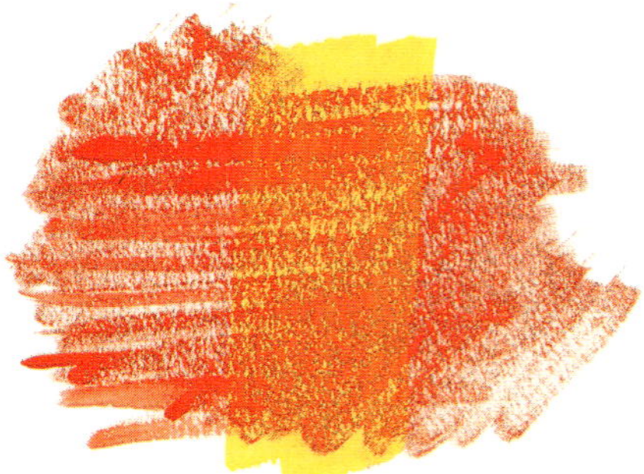

To create texture, use a dry brush by removing excess paint before stroking.

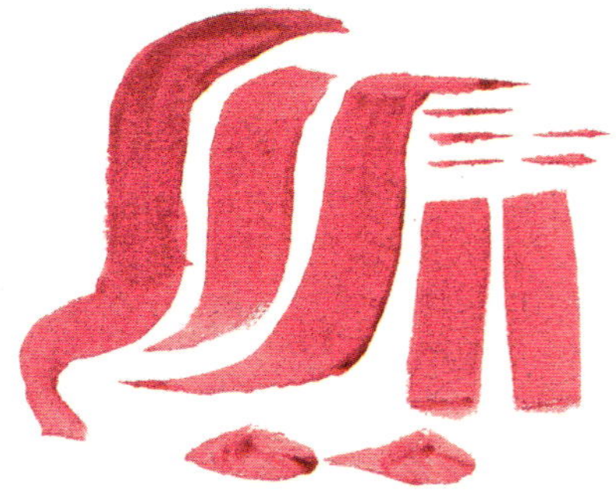

Holding your flat brush at the same angle, change stroke direction to vary the widths.

Create a soft blend by gently overlapping your strokes with a soft, flat brush.

Artist's Tip

Take good care of your brushes: After each painting session, remove excess paint with a paper towel. Then wash your brushes well with soap and water.

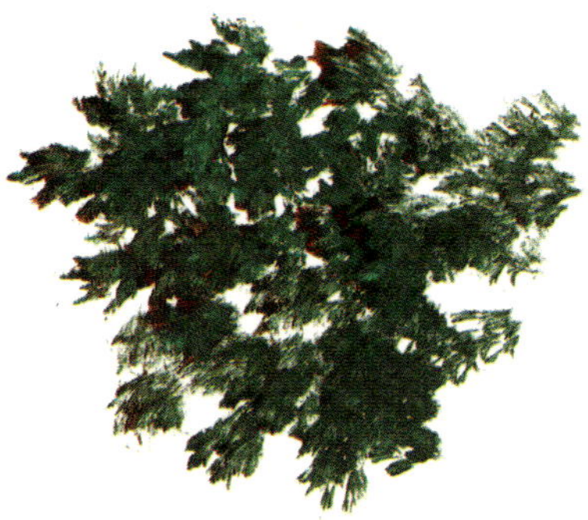

For masses of foliage, spread the tips of a pointed brush and stamp lightly.

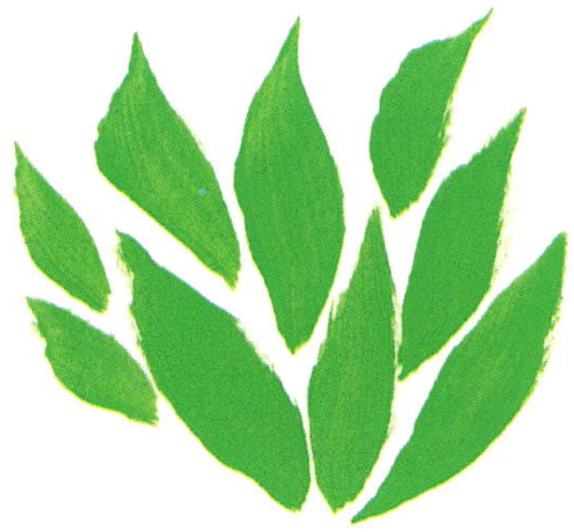

For lush leaves and petals, turn the flat brush without lifting it as you stroke.

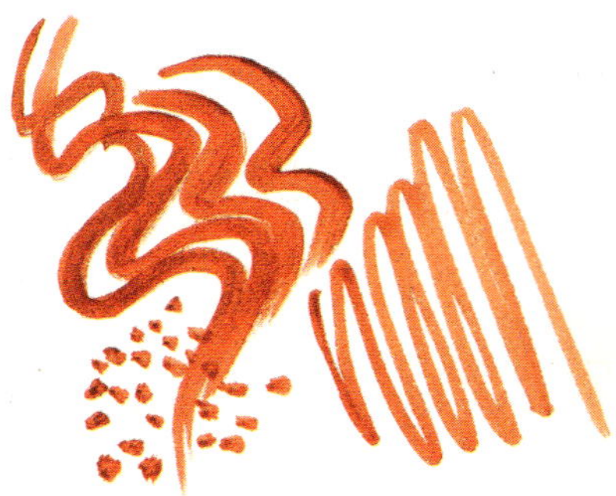

Use the tip of a round brush to render simple lines and dots with precision.

Save Time by Taking Simple Precautions

Acrylic is a great medium for beginners because it dries quickly, which makes it easy to "correct" mistakes. If you want to change the composition or color of a piece, simply paint over it when dry. But it's always best to avoid errors when possible, and some can be prevented from the very beginning. Taking an extra moment to prepare before and while you paint will ensure successful results every time. For example, sketch out your subject before you paint to make sure the sizes and shapes are correct. And keep tools on hand that might be helpful, like a plastic ruler or straightedge you can use as a guide. Thinking ahead will save time and make your painting go smoothly.

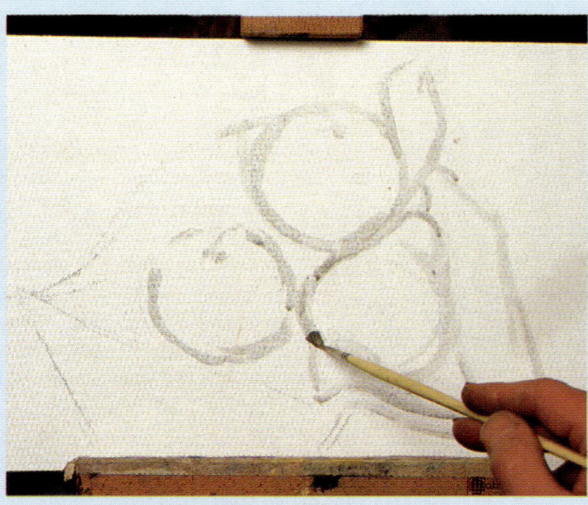

Draw a simple, rough sketch as a guide for your painting. Light pencil is effective, but thinned paint and a small round brush work as well—then you can wash away any errors before you begin your painting.

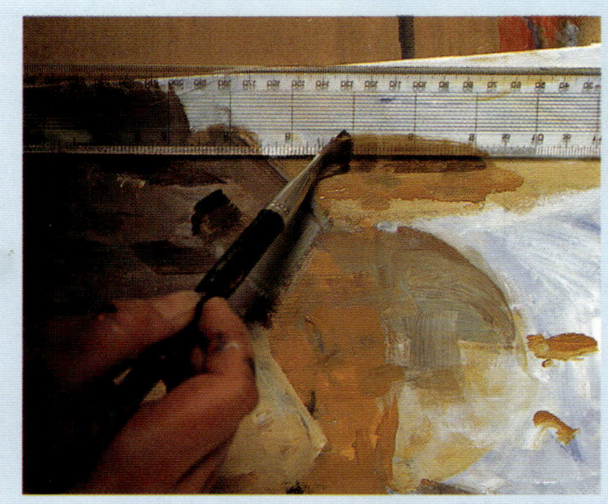

Taking precautions means not leaving things to chance. If your subject requires a perfectly straight line, you can paint against a plastic ruler, a thick sheet of paper, or a strip of masking tape.

FLAT WASH A *flat wash* is a simple way to fill in a large area with a solid color. Load your flat brush with water-diluted paint, and—holding your support at an angle—sweep the color across. Add more paint to your brush between strokes, and let gravity help the strokes together.

GRADED WASH *Graded washes* graduate from dark to light—perfect for water and skies. To create a graded wash, paint horizontal strokes across the top of the tilted painting surface with a flat brush, and add water between strokes to fade out the color gradually.

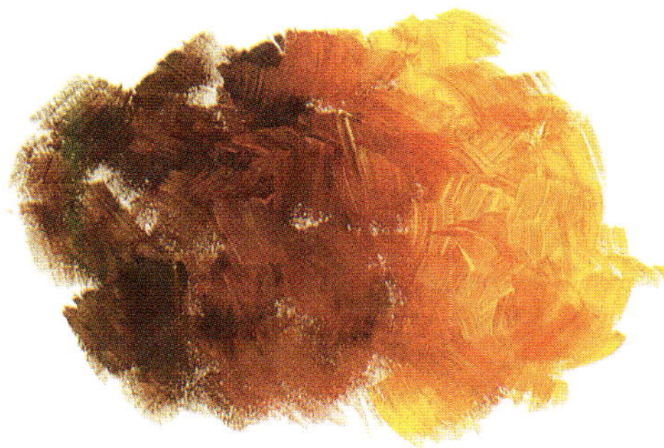

THICK STROKES For more varied color and texture, apply thick paint with a large dry brush. First load a flat brush with burnt sienna. Beginning on the left, lay in the color with short, overlapping strokes, adding cadmium red in the center and cadmium yellow on the right.

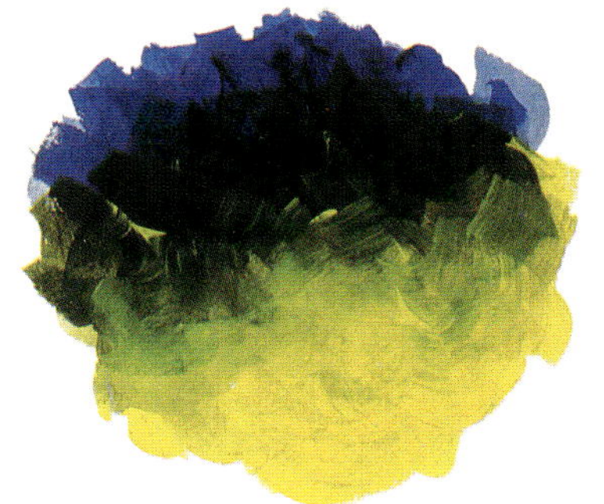

THICK BLENDS You can also create thick color blends by painting with a wet flat brush. Apply a thick layer of yellow paint; then add thick blue brushstrokes. The colors blend where they meet, producing many subtle shades of blue-green, green, and pure blue.

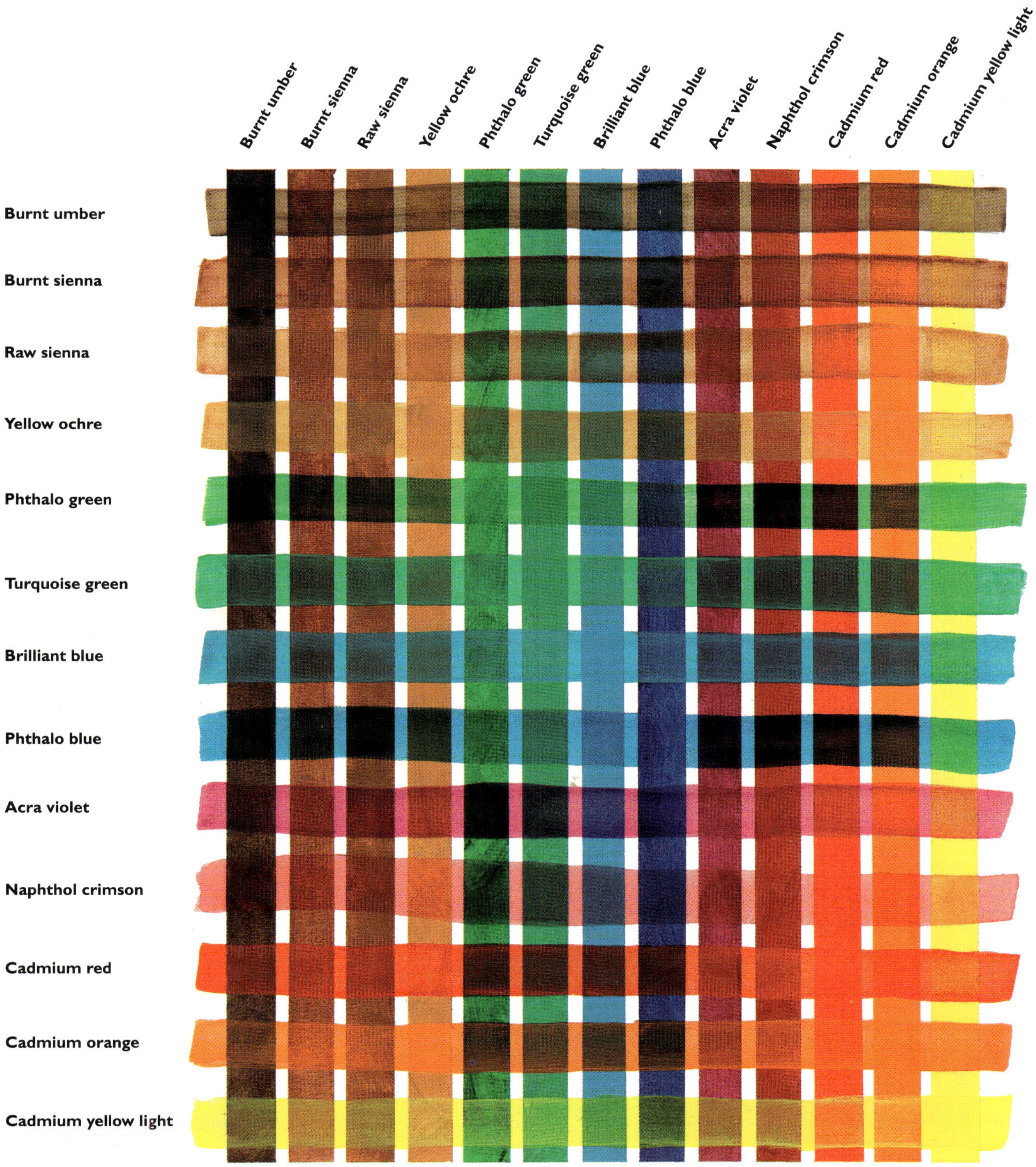

THICK ON THIN Instead of blending, try layering your colors. Apply a thin, transparent wash of paint to establish your "ground," or base color. Then paint thickly on top, leaving gaps to let some of the underpainting show through.

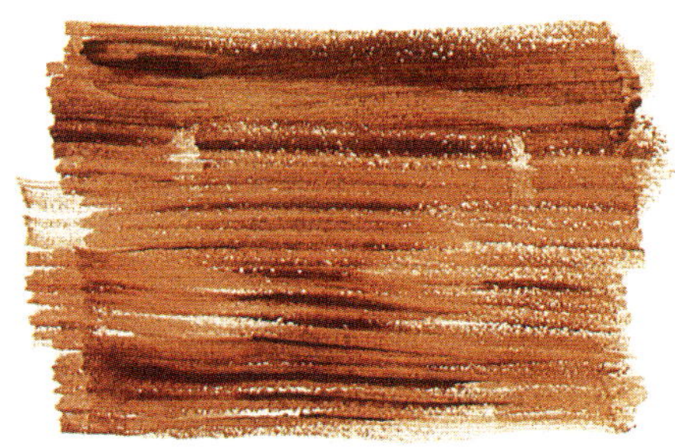

DRY ON WET Pulling dry paint over damp paper makes the colors separate and creates a grainy texture. For this woodlike effect, dip a dry bristle brush in burnt sienna and stroke across the paper.

◄ **MY PALETTE** My palette consists of only thirteen colors (excluding white). This may seem to be a small number at first, but they can create a full range of wonderful possibilities when combined! In this chart, transparent washes of the colors were layered over opaque strokes. Layering with washes (called "glazing"; also see page 25) makes it easy to produce a great array of fascinating, unique shades with a limited number of colors. Make your own chart to familiarize yourself with the color mixing possibilities your palette offers.

Understanding Your Colors

COLOR HAS A TREMENDOUS effect on our feelings and emotions. Red is often thought of as hot and passionate; blue is associated with "cool as ice"; yellow is happy and warm, like sunshine. This means that my choice of colors will determine whether my paintings will seem warm and comfortable, cool and refreshing, or vibrant and dramatic. Knowing the basics of how colors relate to and interact with one another will help you create a mood—and add interest—in all your acrylic paintings.

Choosing Colors to Convey Feelings

Colors are often referred to in terms of warm and cool, which helps make them arouse certain feelings. *Warm* colors (reds, yellows, and oranges) convey energy and excitement; *cool* colors (blues, greens, and purples) are more soothing and peaceful. The "temperature" also varies within each color: a warm red, for example, has more yellow in it, and a cool red has more blue. *Complementary* colors are those that are opposite each other on the color wheel (see the pigment wheel at right). Complements offer a lively contrast when juxtaposed; but when they are mixed, they produce a range of browns and grays *(neutrals)*. Look at the samples on these pages to see how warm, cool, and neutral colors create different moods. Then keep these color schemes in mind when composing your own paintings.

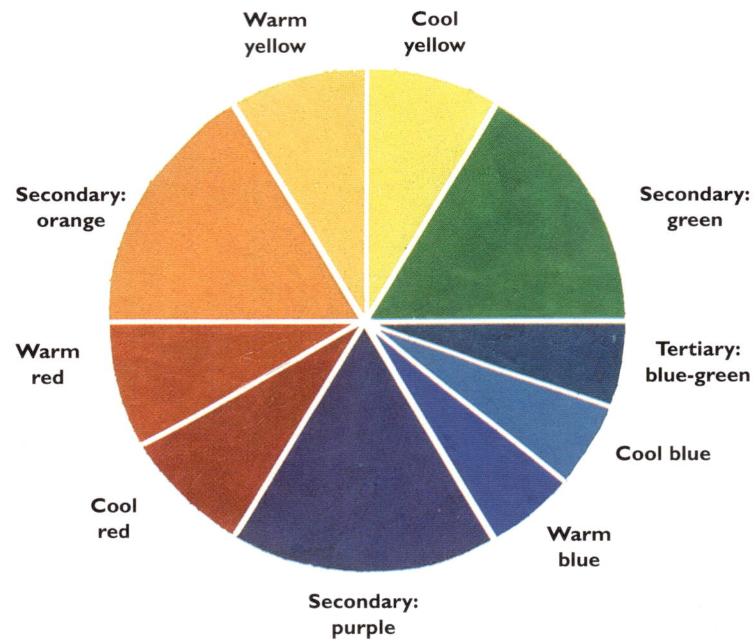

▲ **USING A COLOR WHEEL** **This pigment wheel is a color wheel that demonstrates color relationships, including the difference between warms and cools. The *primaries* (red, blue, and yellow) are the three basic colors that can't be created by mixing other colors. *Secondaries* (orange, green, and purple) are mixes of the adjacent primaries on the wheel; and *tertiaries* are a mix of the adjacent primary and secondary.**

PAINTING IN GRAYS AND NEUTRALS **You don't need to use a lot of brilliant, bright colors in your painting to create mood; neutral colors hold a power of expression all their own. You can mix complementary colors together to create either cool or warm neutrals with a whole range of interesting nuances. The cool, muted colors in the painting at right (see the swatches below for exact color mixes) effectively convey the serenity of this tranquil landscape. Even without adding vivid colors, the contrast of light and dark neutrals make a dramatic painting, full of life and interest.**

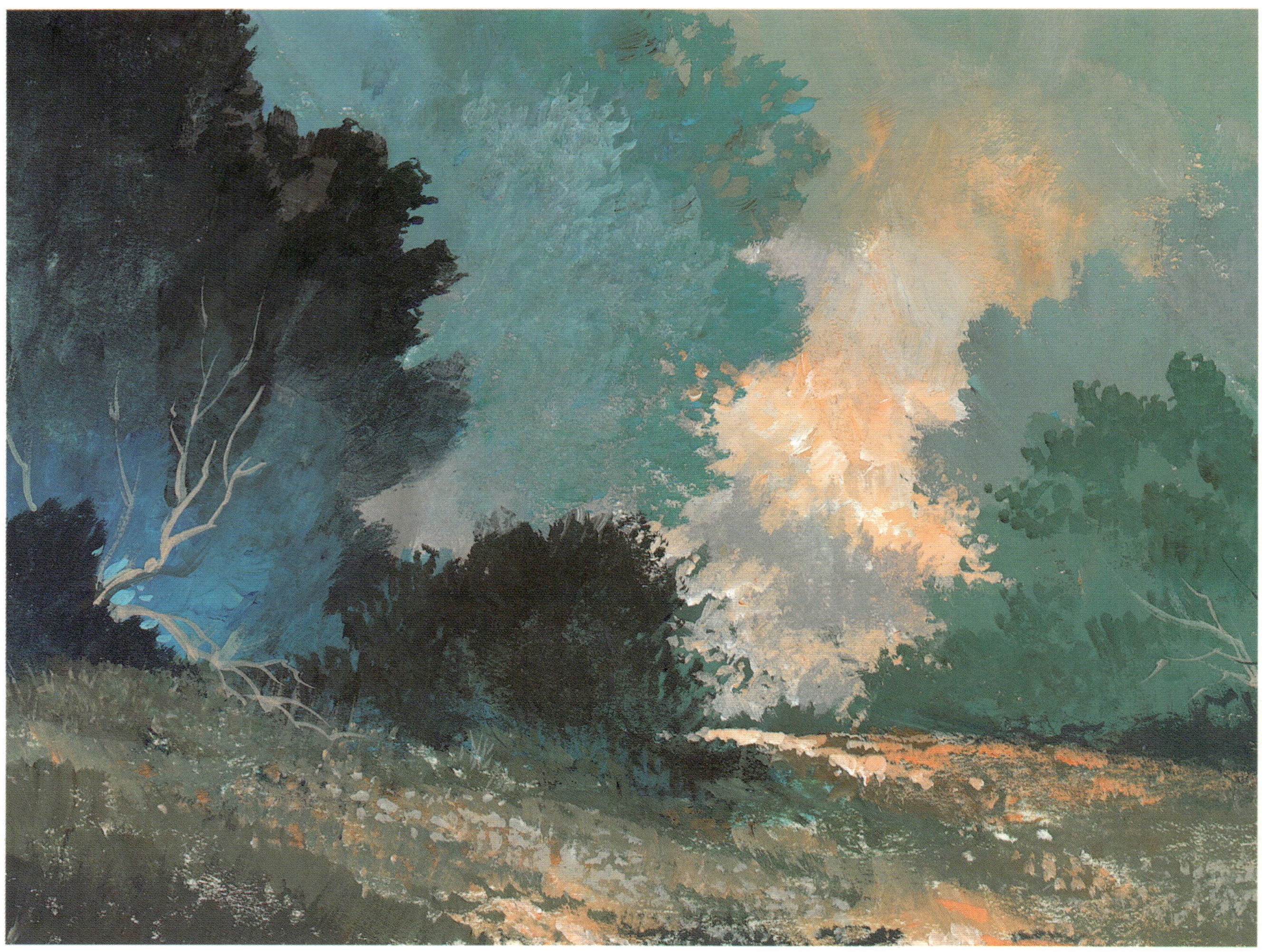

Art by William F. Powell

Artist's Tip

Acrylic darkens as it dries, so before you paint, make some test swatches so you'll know what the colors will look like when they're dry.

MIXING GRAYS

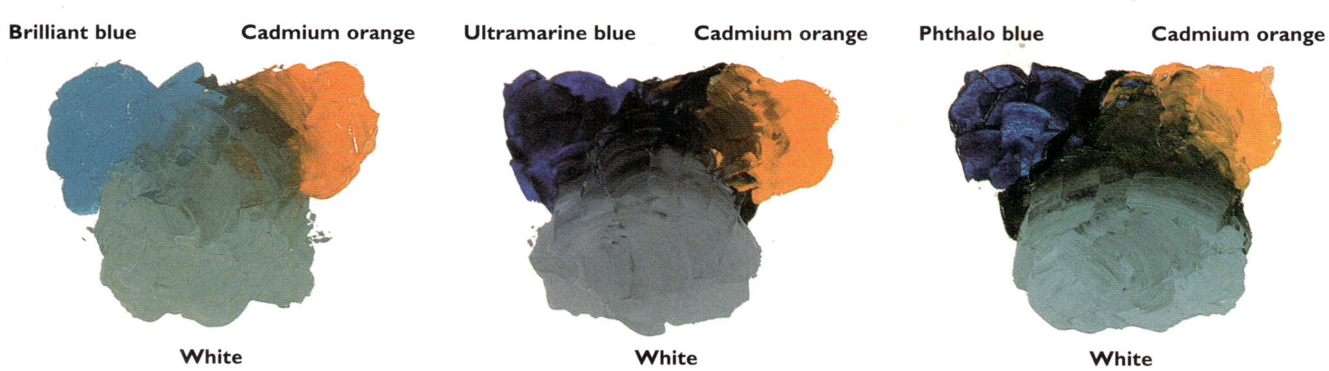

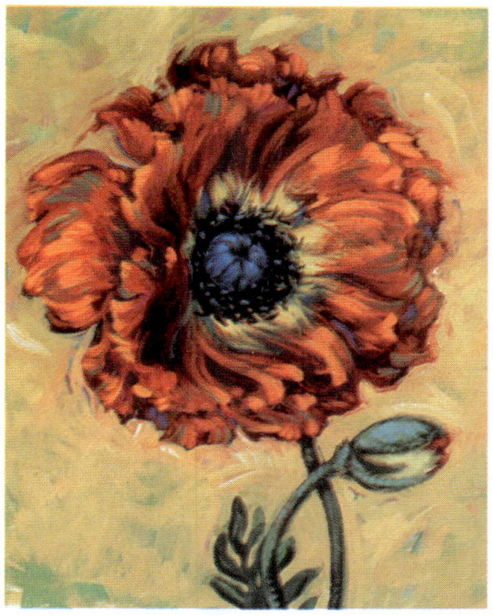

WARM COLORS Warm colors can convey a sense of cheer and comfort or fire and aggression. They are also the most forward—they stand out because our eyes see them as advancing toward us. In this example, the fiery red petals really seem to pop off the canvas.

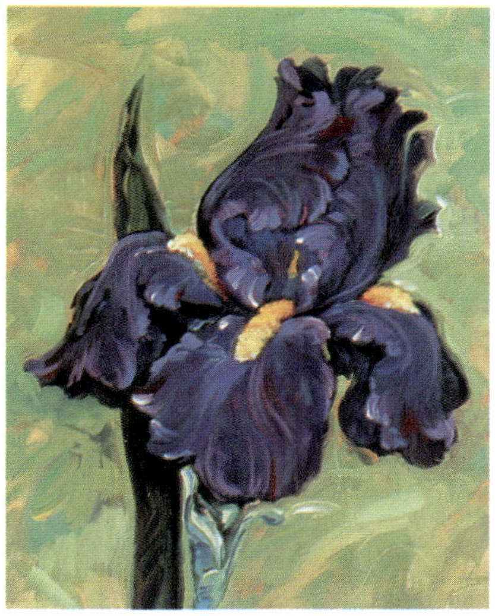

COOL COLORS We tend to associate cool colors with shadows, depth, and quietude. Cool colors also normally retreat from the eye, which makes them good choices for backgrounds and distant objects. Here the blues and purples of the petals have a calm and soothing effect.

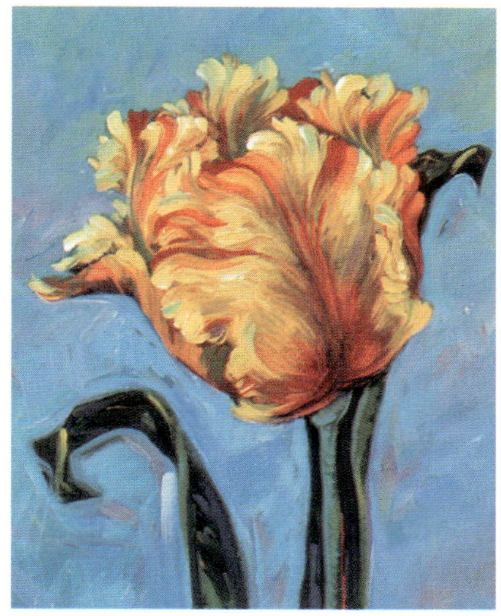

COMPLEMENTARY COLORS Place a color next to its complement whenever you want high drama and a lot of vitality. This combination of a warm orange flower against its cool complement—blue—uses both "temperature" and contrast to rivet attention onto the subject.

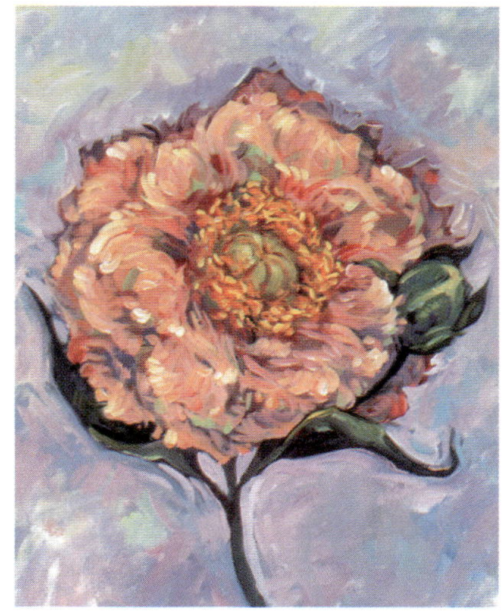

ANALOGOUS COLORS *Analogous* colors are those that are adjacent to one another on the color wheel, like the petals on this peony; they are all various shades of a warm pink. Because these colors are all similar to one another, they create a sense of unity and harmony.

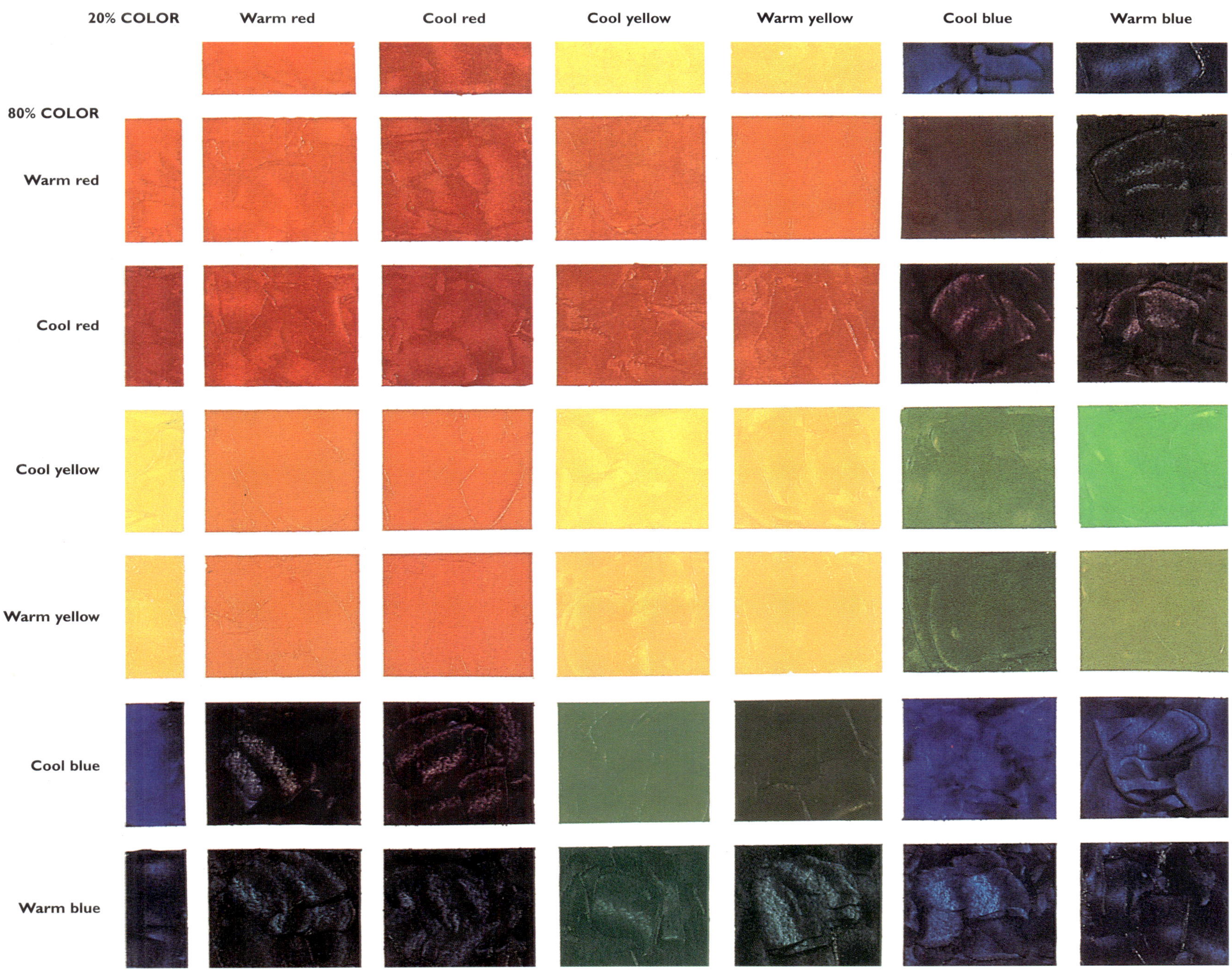

MIXING COLORS In theory, you can mix every color you might need from the three primaries—red, yellow, and blue. But all primaries are not created alike, so you'll need to have at least two versions of each primary available to work with, one warm (containing more red) and one cool (containing more blue). As shown on the chart above, the two primary sets give you a wide range of secondary mixes. You'll also find that they produce a generous array of subtle, neutral shades when mixed.

Approaching the Painting

EVERY BLANK CANVAS IS FULL of exciting possibilities, and choosing a subject is one of my favorite things about painting! Many things inspire me, but I really enjoy painting my surroundings. For example, I draw some of my greatest inspirations from the New England coast and countryside; it's filled with scenic views and intriguing subjects. Find things that inspire you in your own life—your children, your garden, your favorite pet, last summer's vacation photos, or your own region's natural wonders.

Getting Started

Once you've picked a subject, getting started is easy to do. It's just a matter of breaking down the painting into a series of simple steps, as demonstrated in this painting of a line of boats at dock. Whether working from life or from a photo reference, I always start with a sketch to establish the basic shapes of my subject; then I gradually build up layers of color and finish with a few details.

► WORKING FROM A PHOTO Painting on site is a wonderful experience, but it isn't always practical. I came upon this charming scene one day and took a photo for future reference. I especially liked the dramatic viewpoint, so I used a wide-angle lens to emphasize it even further.

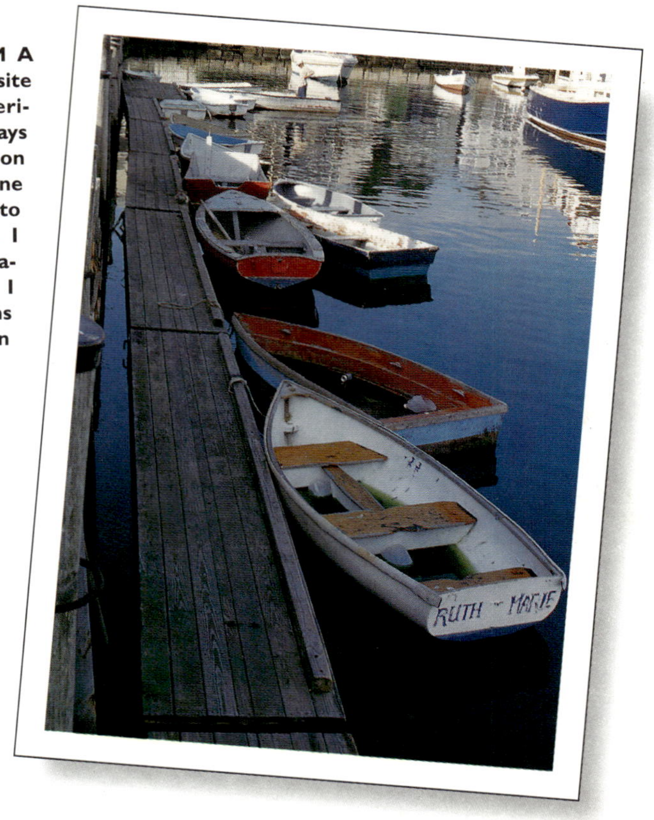

1 I begin each painting with a pencil sketch directly on my illustration board. I start by lightly drawing a few guidelines—the angle of the pier and the placement of each boat—and then I draw the outlines of each object. As I sketch, I constantly check the size relationships, or *proportions,* of the elements in relation to one another: How long is the boat compared to its width? How much larger is the boat in the foreground compared to the boats in the distance? Then I refine all the main outlines (ignoring the fine details for now) so I have a clear "map" for placing all my colors.

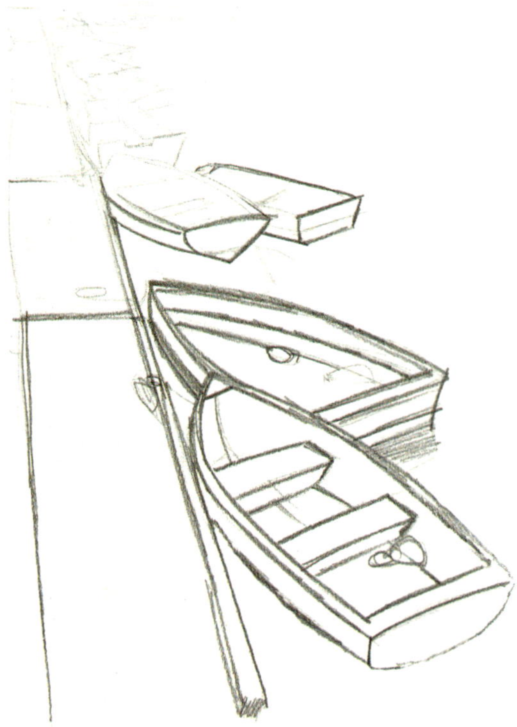

2 I'm going to start with dark washes of color for the water around the boats, and I don't want to lose the light pencil lines under my base color. So, working quickly with a small brush and thin paint, I outline the boats in black and lay in black and burnt umber for the pier. Next I start at the base of the canvas with a wash of cool acra violet and phthalo blue for the darkest water color. Then I wash in pure cool phthalo blue in the center, and I progress to a warmer turquoise green as I move up toward the sunlit area of the water. My objective is to create a strong contrast between the cool shadows in the foreground and the warmer colors in the background.

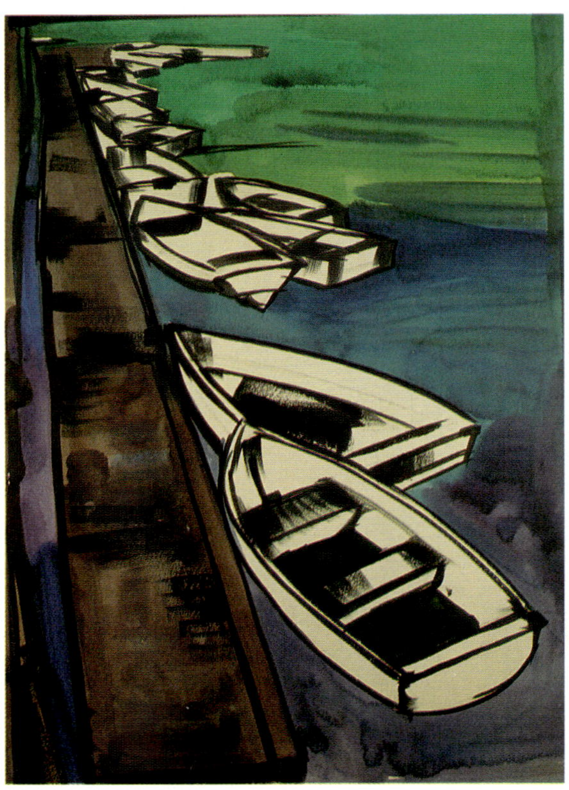

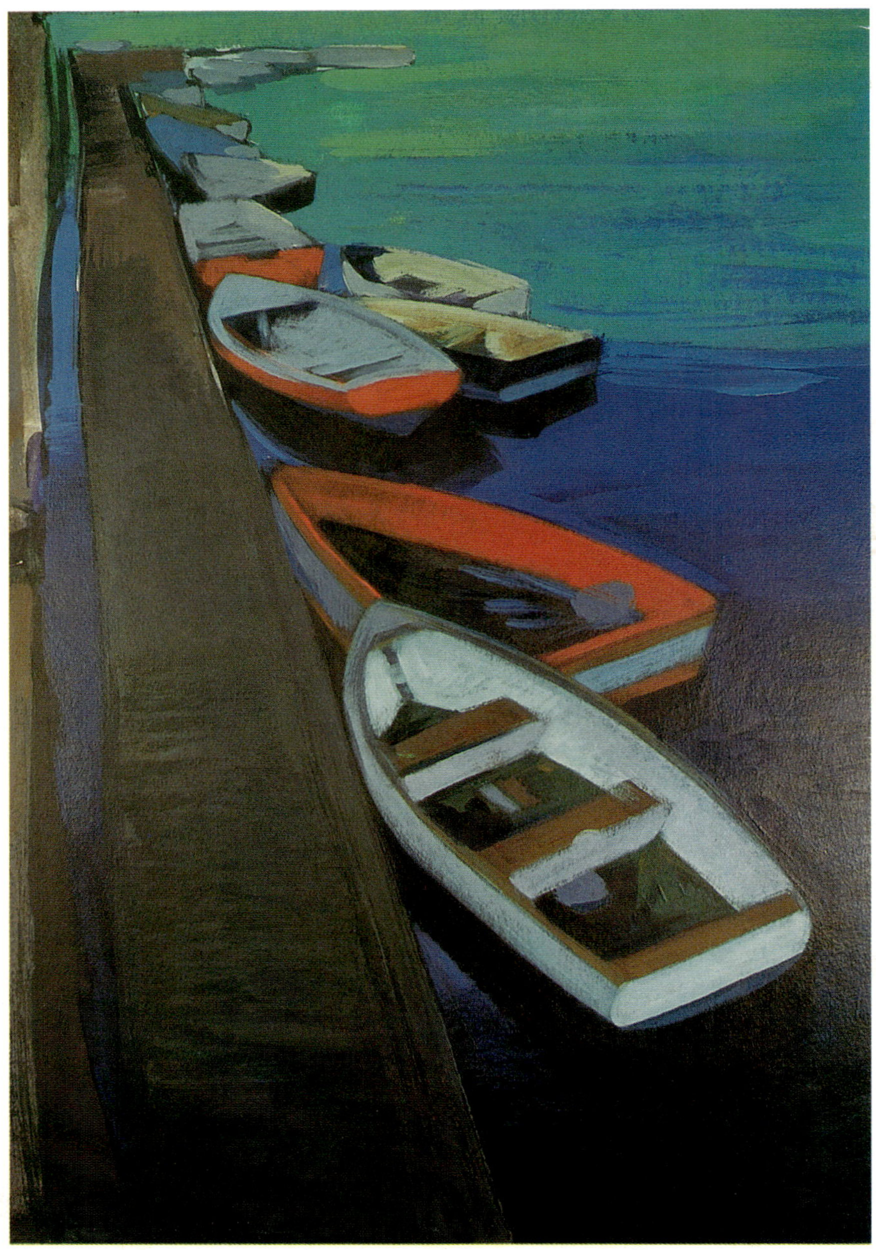

3 Next I apply the base color on the boats with warm reds and cool shadows. To keep attention away from the decking, I paint it a deep purple-gray (burnt umber, phthalo blue, and acra violet). Then I build up the graded color of the water by patiently painting layer on layer of subtly different shades of blues and turquoise using a bristle brush.

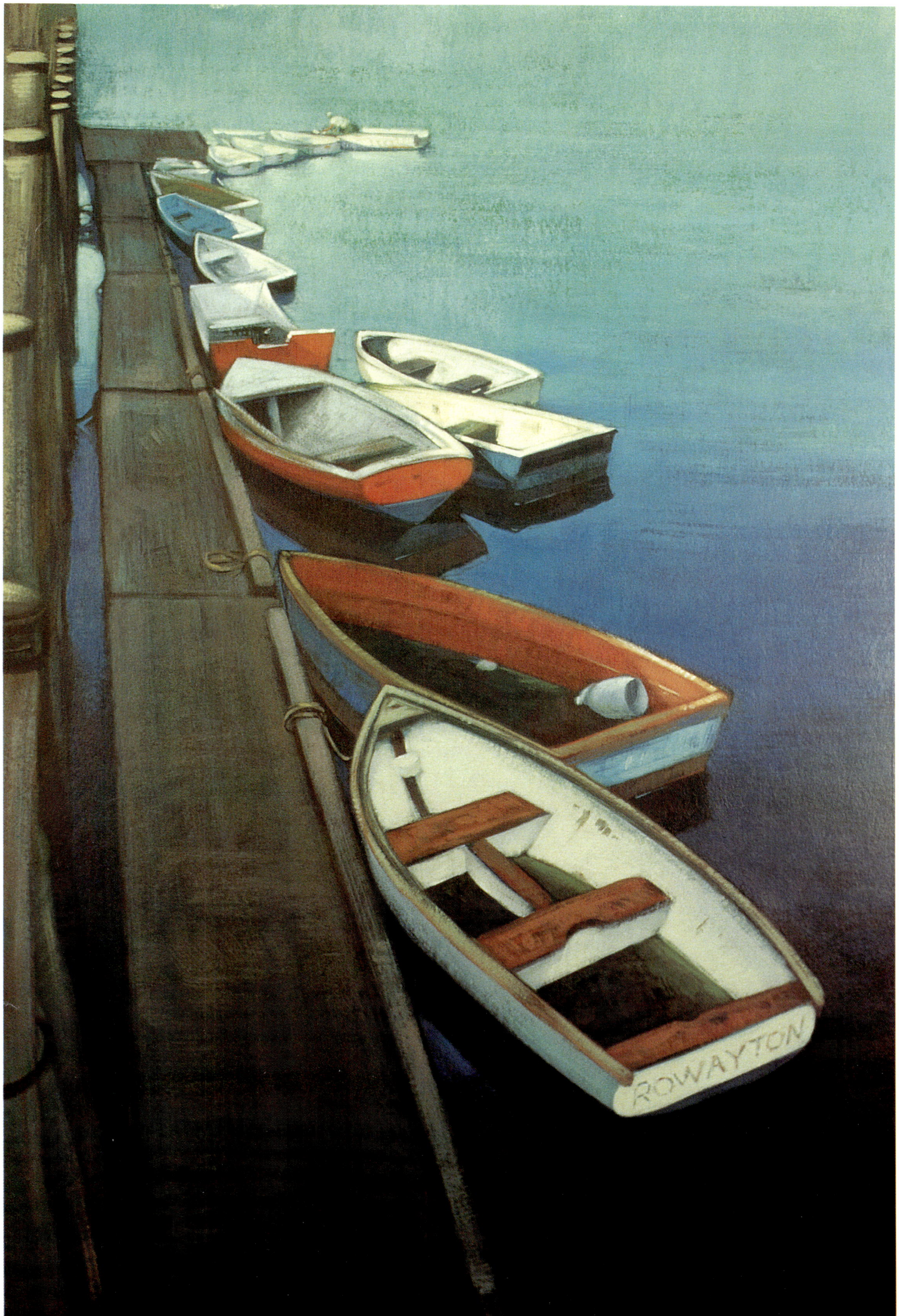

4 I continue building up layers of increasingly lighter colors until I am satisfied with the water. Then I refine the lines and shadows on the boats and the decking and add the details. For the final touches, I add white highlights to show where the sunlight flickers onto the boats using a small round brush and a mix of almost pure titanium white warmed with just a touch of cadmium yellow light.

▼ LIGHT WATER MIXES
Phthalo blue and turquoise green, with varying amounts of white and a speck of cadmium yellow light for the lightest areas

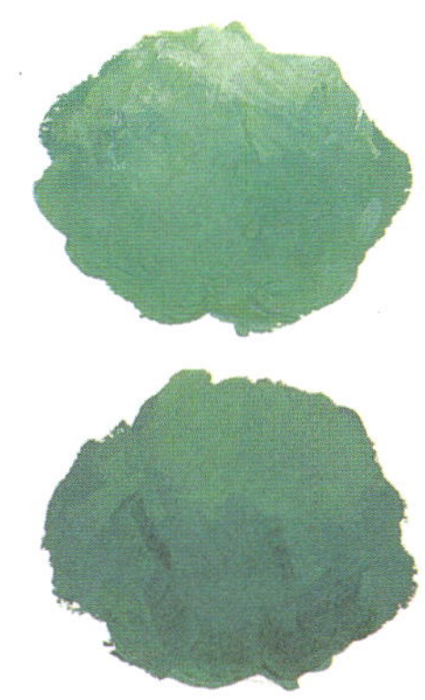

▼ MEDIUM WATER MIXES
Phthalo blue, turquoise green, and varying amounts of white

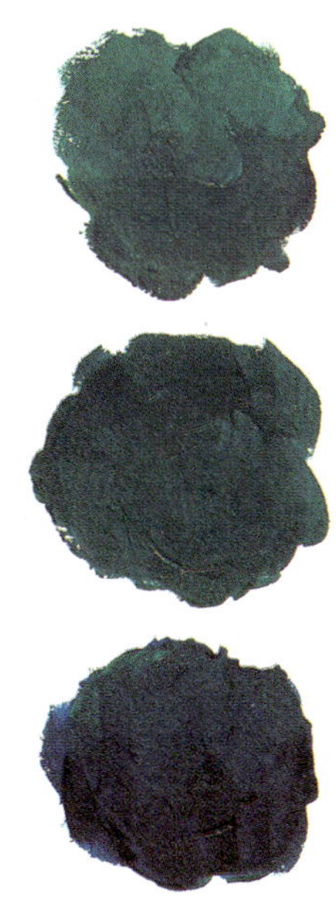

▼ DARK WATER MIXES
Phthalo blue and acra violet

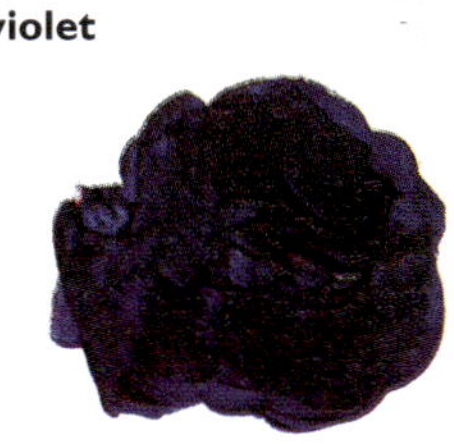

Composing the Subject

ONCE YOU'VE DECIDED ON A SUBJECT to paint, the next step is to create a pleasing *composition*. I like to think of composition as organization—it's simply the process of finding an interesting and balanced arrangement of the subject matter. A good composition leads the viewer's eye around the painting through the use of interesting shapes, diagonals, and curving lines, creating a visual path that leads the eye to the center of interest, or *focal point*. As I set up my composition, I make sure not to place the focal point directly in the middle of the painting—I can create a much more dynamic scene by placing the focal point slightly off-center, as you can see in the examples on these pages.

1 Here I took elements of both reference photos and sketched out my own composition. I placed the focal point (the men at the front of the boat) just to the left of center and created a diagonal line of action to draw the eye in—and give it someplace interesting to go. Imagine how sedentary this composition would have been if the subjects were simply arranged straight across the page!

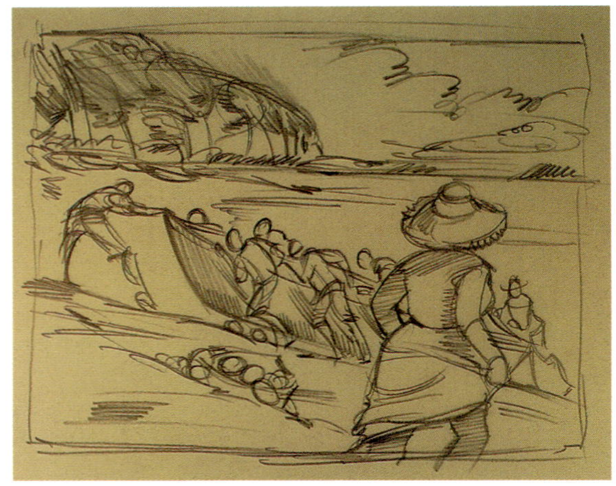

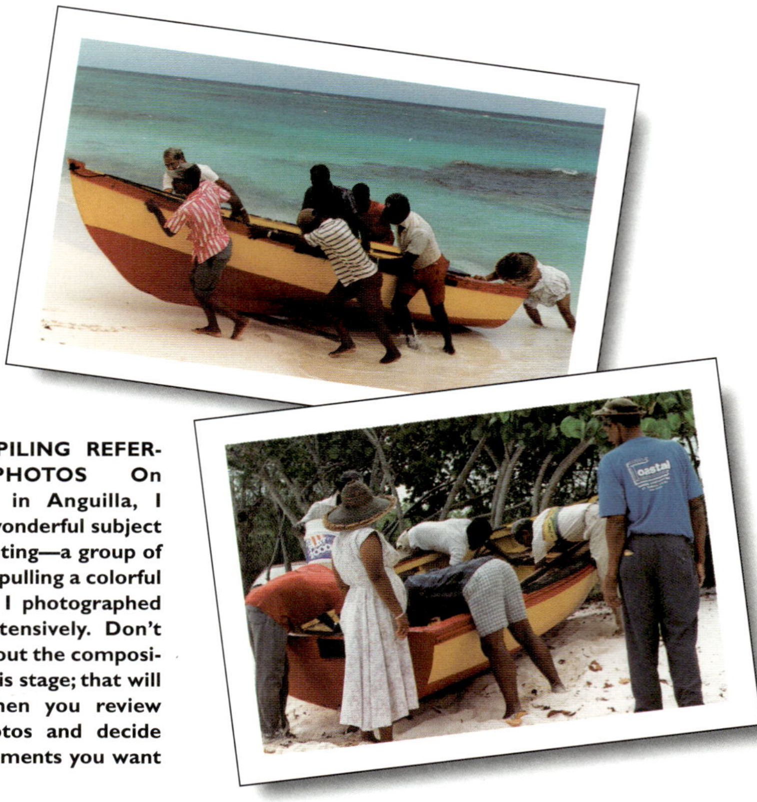

▶ **COMPILING REFERENCE PHOTOS** On vacation in Anguilla, I found a wonderful subject for a painting—a group of islanders pulling a colorful boat—so I photographed them extensively. Don't worry about the composition at this stage; that will come when you review your photos and decide which elements you want to paint.

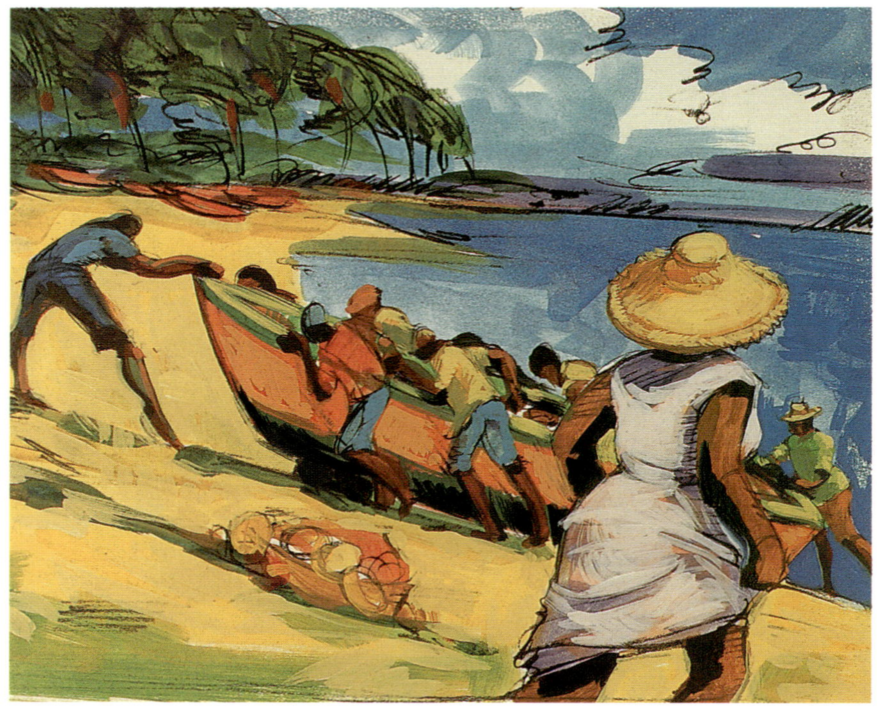

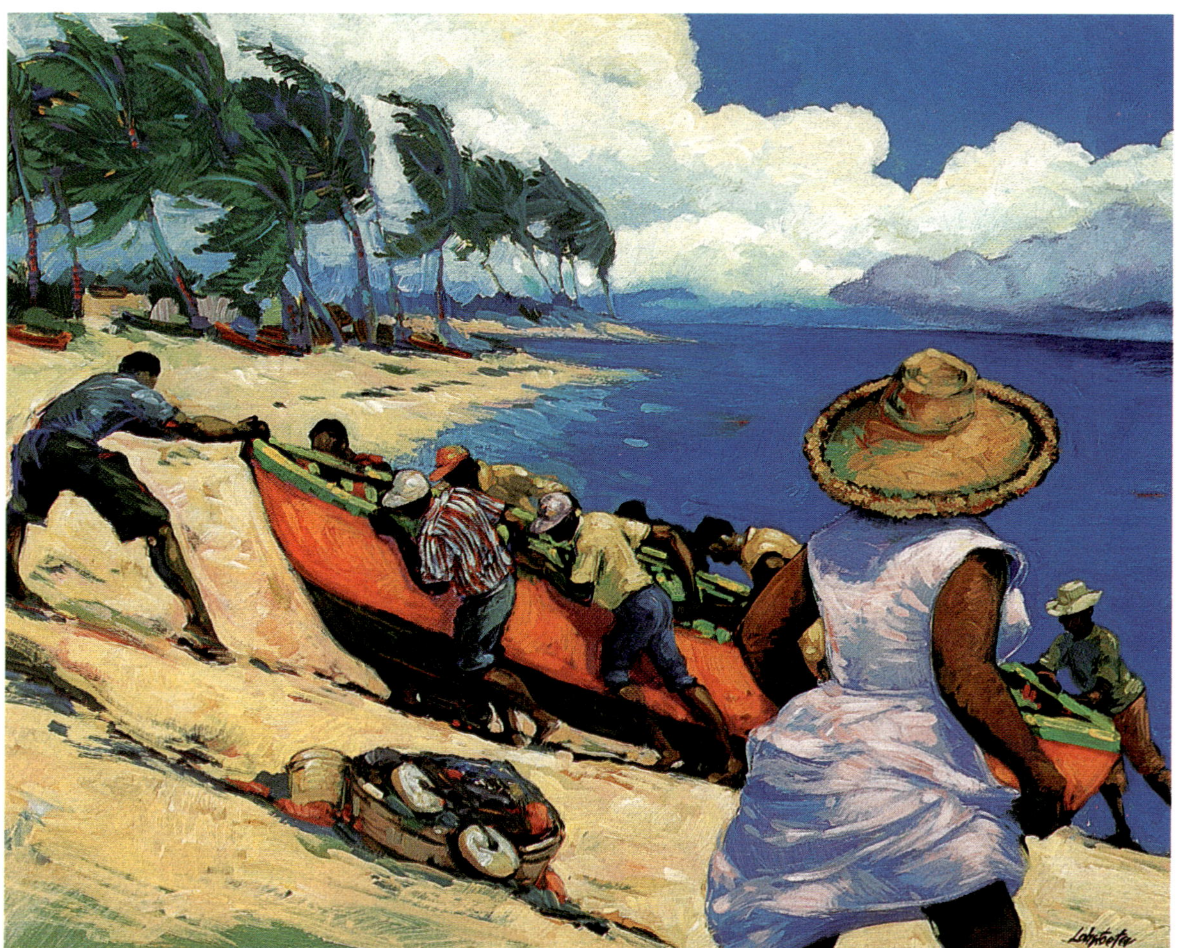

2 Now I begin blocking in the base colors (the underpainting). I love the brilliant colors I can mix with acrylic, and I take advantage of the medium to punch up the colors in the whole scene. Then I consider the balance of color in the overall composition. Do the colors draw the eye to my focal point? Do I need more color anywhere to pull in the viewer? Is any area too overpowering? If so, I make the adjustments in the next step.

3 Now I build up layers of color to give my subjects form (see pages 12–13 for more on form and shading) and add the finishing details. Notice the balance of color in this painting: The mass of light sand is echoed in the billowy white clouds, and the large figure in white in the foreground balances the left side of the composition. She also serves as an entry point for the viewer's eye, and her body position leads the viewer up the diagonal line of boaters to the bow of the eye-popping red boat.

Combining References

To get the most pleasing composition, I often combine elements from my reference file (also referred to as an *artist's morgue*) of photos and pictures that appeal to me. I might use the sky from one photo, a figure from another, and some background foliage from yet another, as I did for my painting of boaters in Anguilla. I may even change the entire color scheme to match the mood I want to convey. This is a wonderful part of the creative process, and it ensures that each painting I create is completely original.

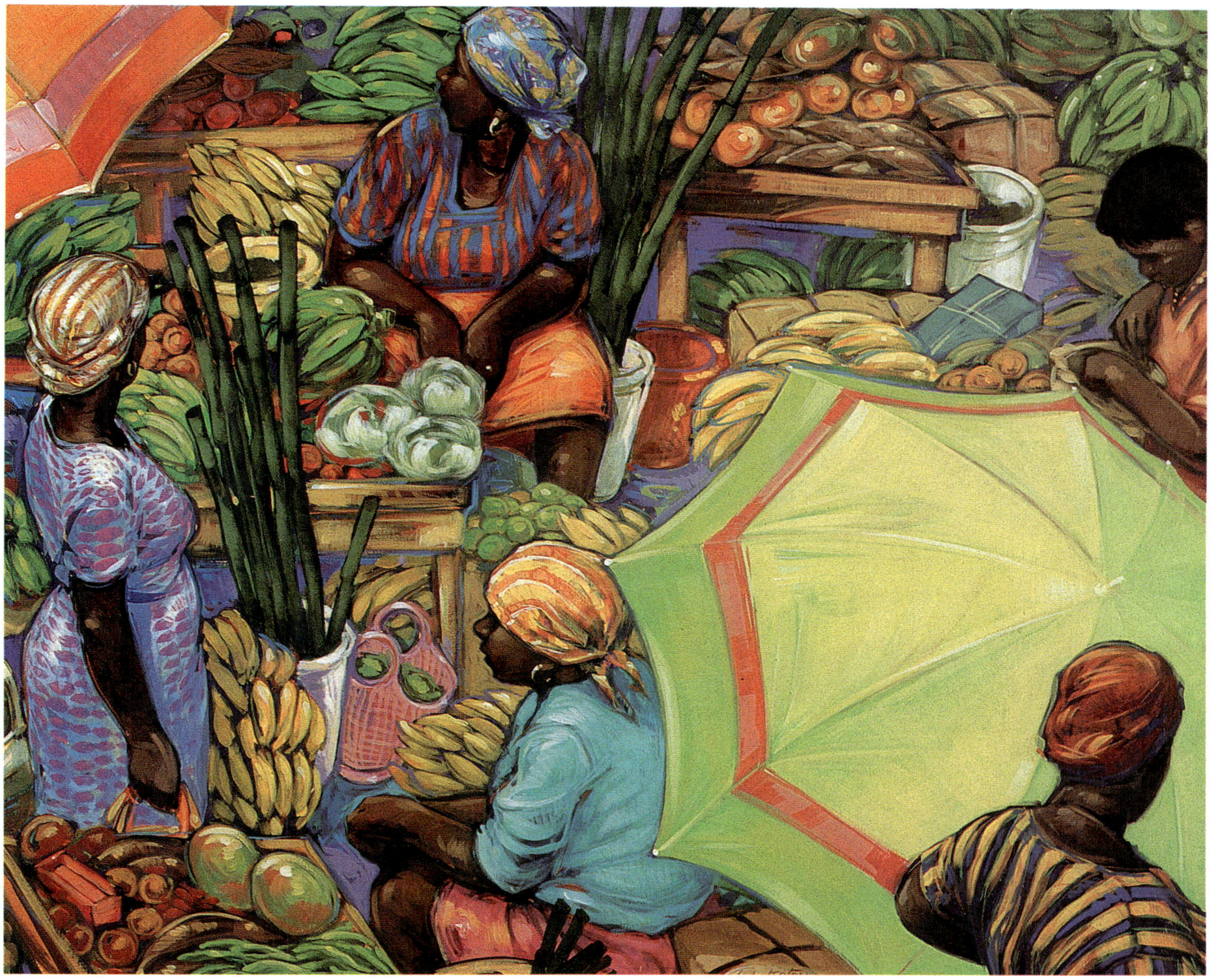

3 As I finish building the colors and adding details, I adjust my brushstrokes to fit my subject. In this painting, the figures are the most solid and well-defined elements: All the other objects are treated with looser brushwork. The large umbrella in the foreground is a flatter expanse of solid color, giving the eye a break from all the details of the marketplace. And repeating the same shape in the umbrella in the upper left corner helps to balance the whole composition—and keep your eye from wandering right out of the picture field!

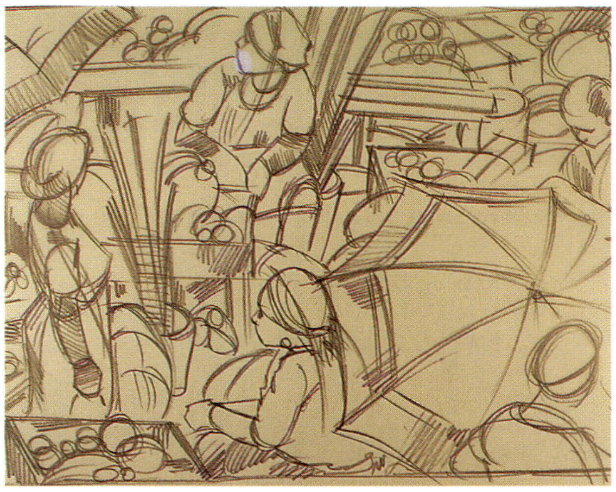

1 This is a somewhat complex scene because I want to capture the hustle and bustle of the colorful marketplace. I place my center of interest—the woman surrounded by fruit—just off-center and high in the picture field. The curved line of figures, the repetition of round shapes, the vertical plants, and even the points of the umbrella all lead the eye into the painting, through it, and toward the center of interest.

2 I want the palette for this marketplace to be very bright and colorful. To block in this scene, I start with a light yellow wash over the entire board, knowing that this underpainting will influence every color I layer on top of it and will shine through between the details. Then I block in the colors of the basic shapes of each element, pairing complements for vibrancy and excitement. Notice that the warm reds and yellows really pop forward, while the cool, blue shadows recede.

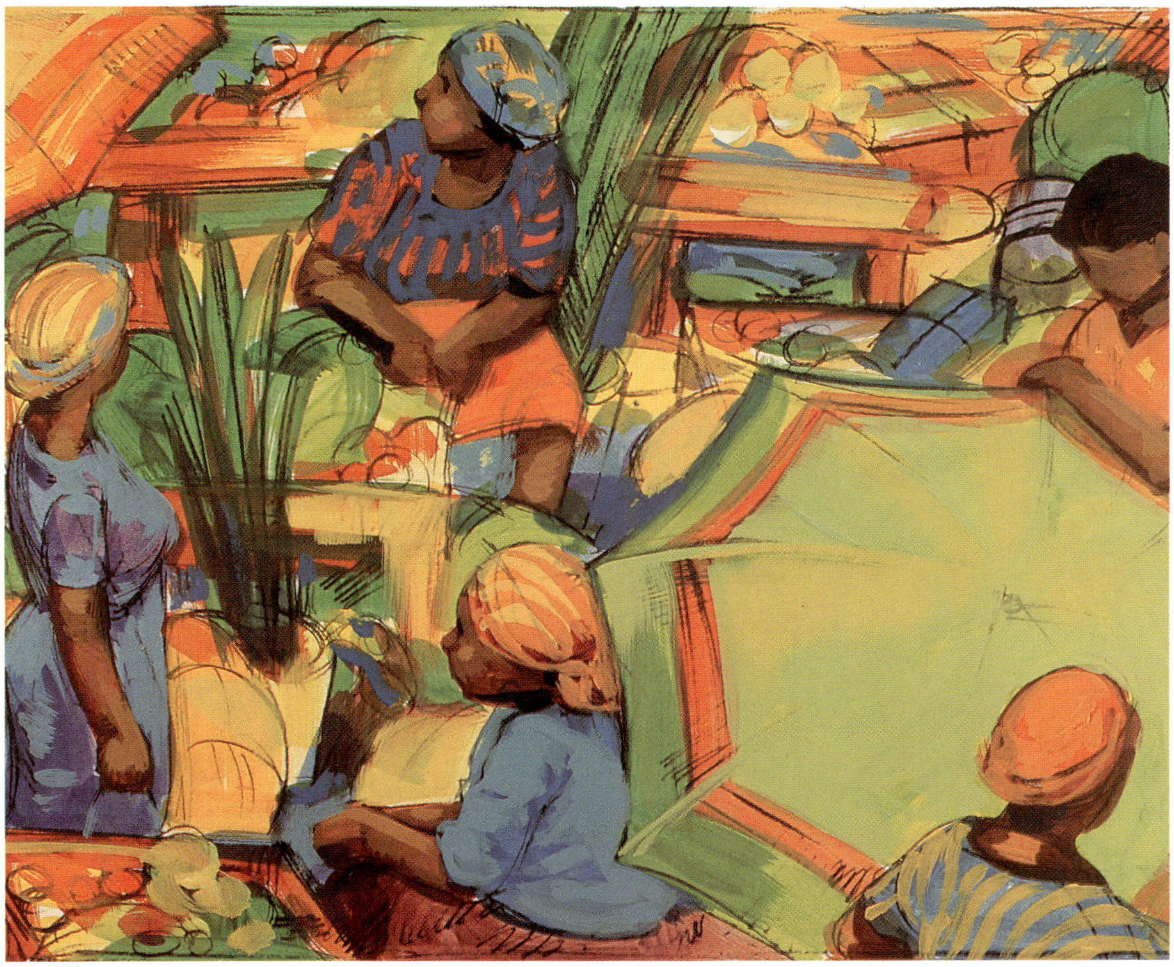

Rendering Form

WHETHER YOUR SUBJECT is a green boat or a red apple, it has a color you can readily identify. It also has a basic *shape* (its outline) and *form* (depth and dimension). I've found that it's easy to paint anything I want if I first break it down into basic shapes: circles, squares, rectangles, and triangles. For example, boats are triangles and rectangles, and apples are basically circles. Then I add the light and dark variations caused by light and shadow, and my subject has form!

Using Values to Model Form

How do you make something look three-dimensional? *Value* is the term that describes the relative lightness or darkness of a color (including black), and it's the variation of values that gives the illusion of form. The apples in the simple still life on these pages are a great exercise in rendering form, but before you start, study the shadow example below, and then practice looking at things in terms of values. Squint your eyes; that blurs all the details and lets you focus on the lights and darks. Notice where the light is coming from and where the darkest shadows are. The more you learn to see, the better your paintings will be!

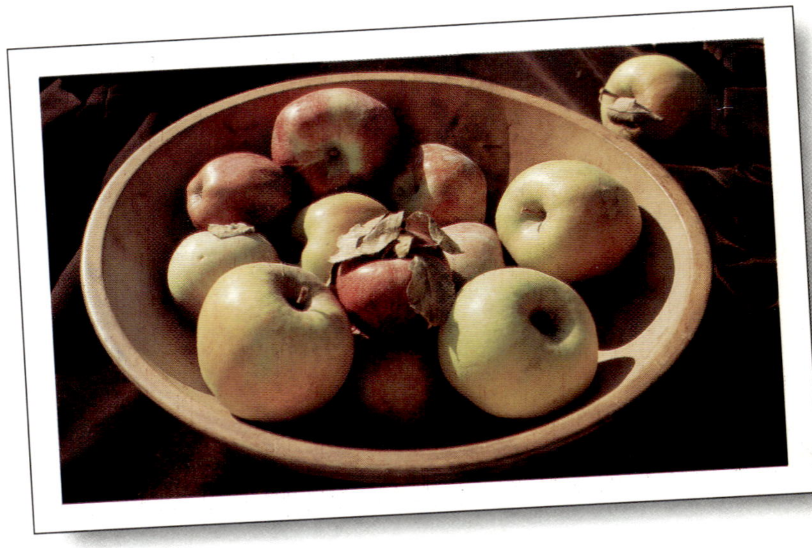

▲ SETTING UP A STILL LIFE Still lifes offer wonderful opportunities for studying shape and form. Kitchen and household items come in a range of basic shapes, and they are readily available subjects. (And they won't move while you're painting!) For this lesson, I used a strong light source to create dramatic shadows and to emphasize the contrasts between the light and dark values.

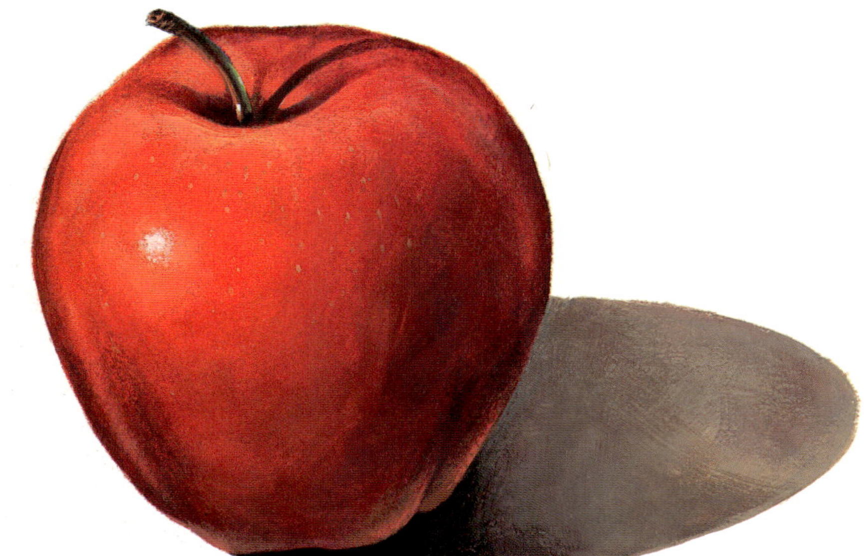

Detail art by William F. Powell

▲ UNDERSTANDING SHADOWS There are two distinct types of shadows: *form* shadows are those on the objects themselves, creating the object's dark values. The *cast* shadows are the dark shadows the object throws onto another surface. The form shadows have soft, blended edges, whereas the cast shadows are often hard-edged.

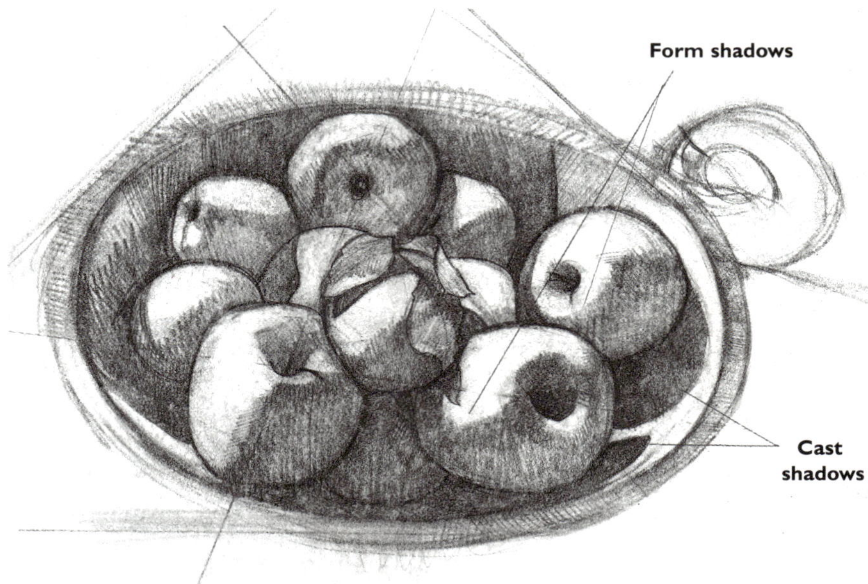

▲ SKETCHING IN VALUES I like to plan out my values with a monochromatic (one-color) sketch before I begin painting. The sketch helps me concentrate on values without having to worry about color as well. I make a simple drawing, concentrating on the main areas of lights and darks that define my subject's form.

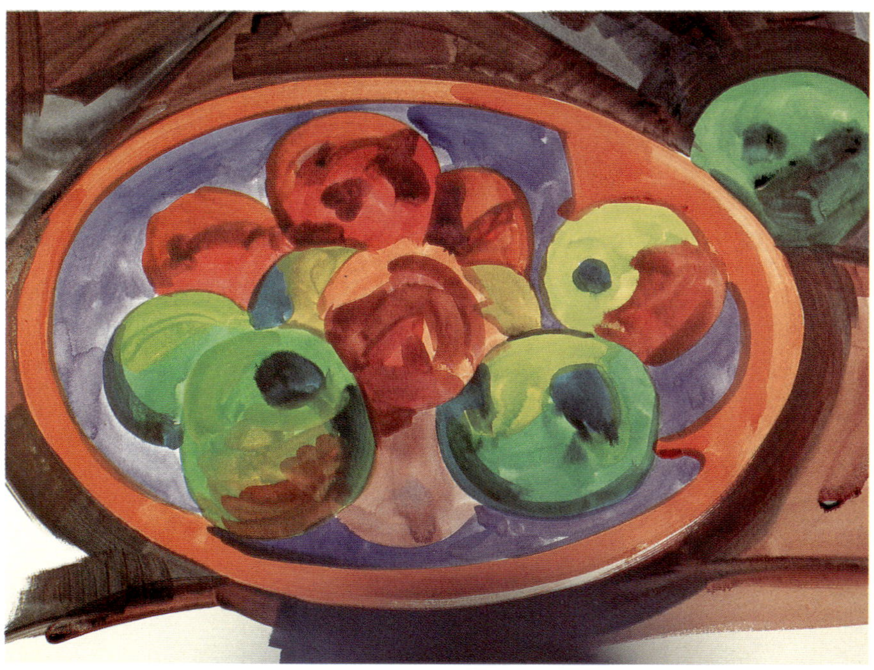

1 I begin with washes of color for the middle values: cadmium red and naphthol crimson for the red apples and cadmium yellow light and phthalo green for the greens. For the form shadows on the green apples, I add a hint of phthalo blue. Then I paint a warm red bowl and wash in a background of burnt umber, acra violet, and brilliant blue.

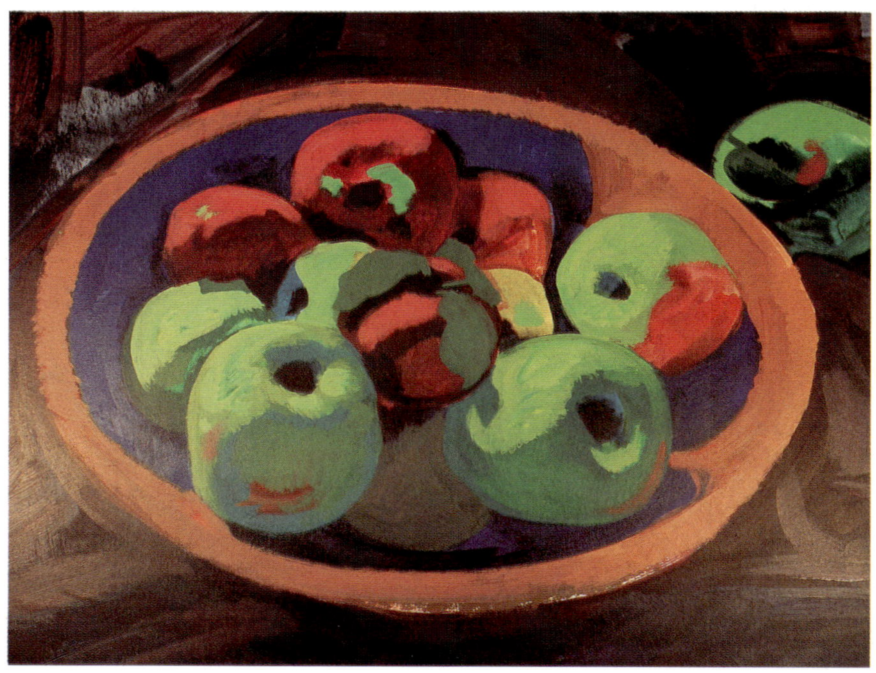

2 With a medium round brush, I reinforce my darks and lights with a thicker paint mix, pushing up the colors. I enhance the bottom of the green apples where the light reflects by adding a touch of brilliant blue to the shadows. Then I mix some of the greens and reds from the apples into the cast shadows in the front section of the bowl.

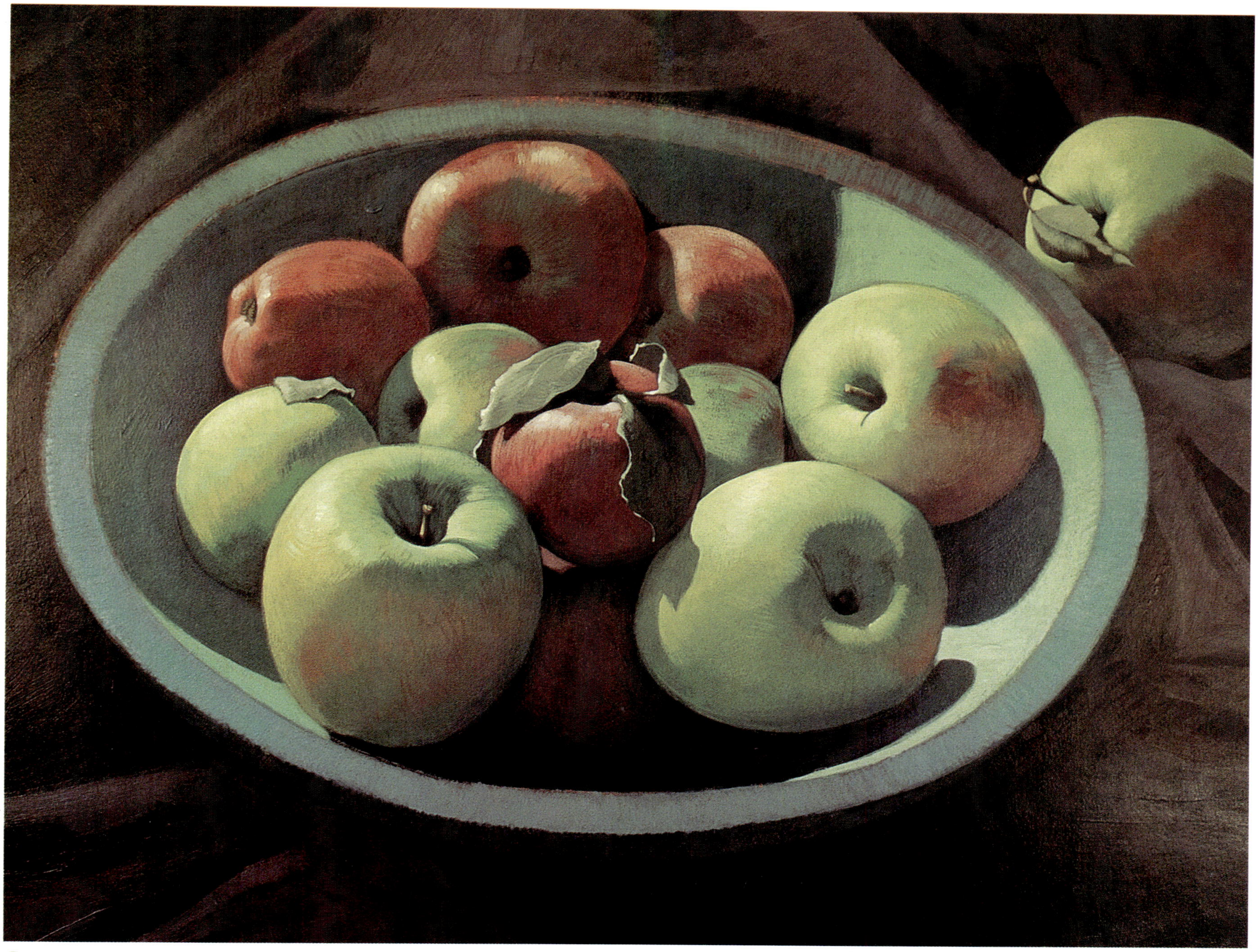

4 With a small round brush, I intensify the shadows and boost the highlights. Then I emphasize the inner curve of the bowl with turquoise-green, cadmium yellow light, and white.

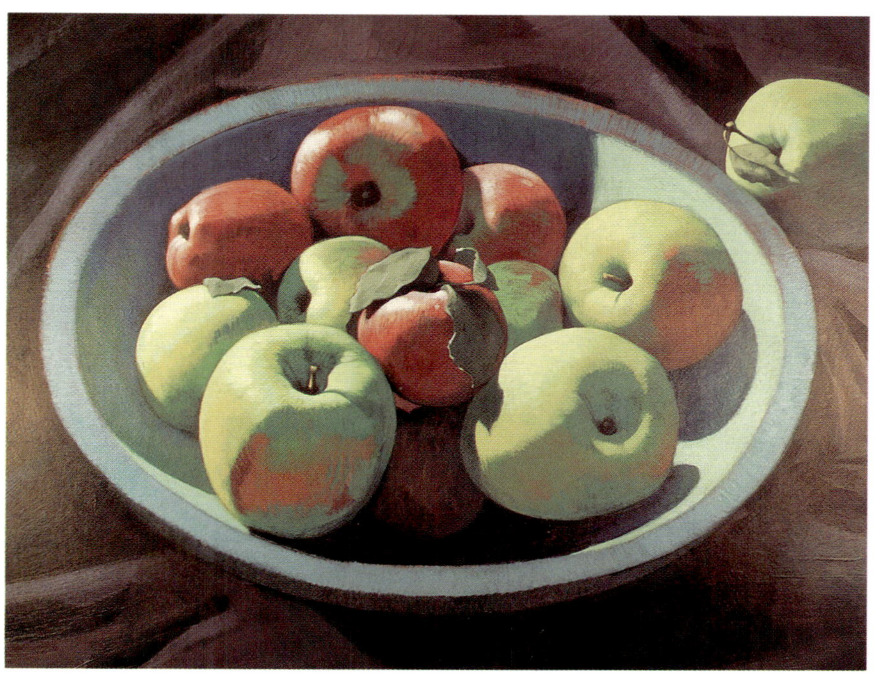

3 As I build up the forms of the apples and the bowl, I stroke the brush in the direction of their shapes, rounding the apples and flattening the rim of the bowl (see the detail for an explanation of the color shift). Using a large flat bristle brush, I build up my dark background with burnt umber, acra violet, phthalo blue, and a little white.

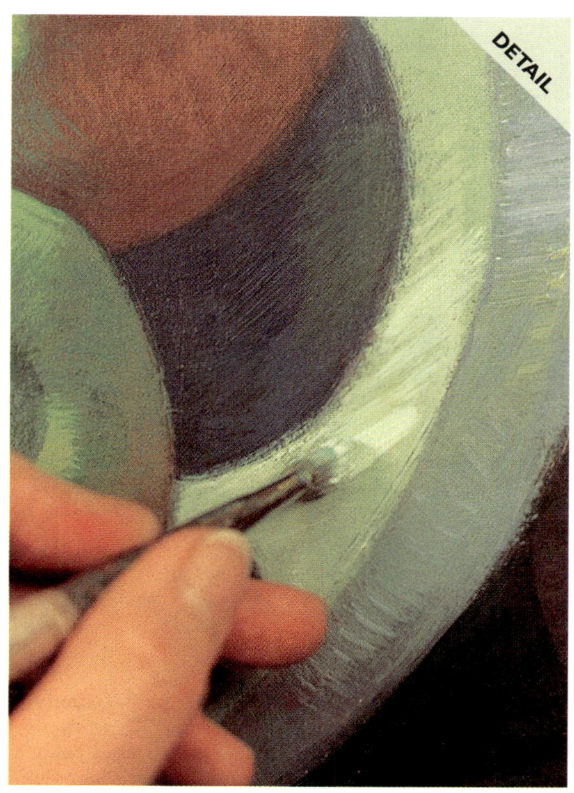

◀ **MAKING COLOR DECISIONS** I originally painted in a warm red bowl, but I very much wanted to keep my cool blue shadows, so I decided to change the bowl's color. It's easy to do with acrylic—I simply painted over the dried paint! I chose a coolish gray color for the bowl, adding hints of mint green and purple. To develop its form, I change my brushstrokes as needed to follow the direction of the different planes of the bowl.

Capturing Time of Day

LIGHT IS A POWERFUL ELEMENT in a painting; it can make colors appear dull and gray, pale and washed out, or vibrant and rich. Just as artificial light can make shadows appear soft or harsh, the strength and angle of the sun can affect the shadows in an outdoor scene. For example, the studies on page 15 show how the highlights and shadows appear at different times of the day. With just a subtle change of color and shadows, my paintings can convey the coolness of morning, the heat of mid-day, or the waning warmth of a late afternoon.

Depicting Dusk

I'm especially fond of the vibrant colors present in the "golden hour," or dusk. There's often a dramatic contrast between the bright, warm patches of light and the long, cool shadows as the sun goes down. In my painting of empty Adirondack chairs on the sand, I used the warm sunset colors, the golden light on the sand, and the calm water to convey a sense of quiet and peaceful solitude—a relaxing time when all the beachgoers have gone away.

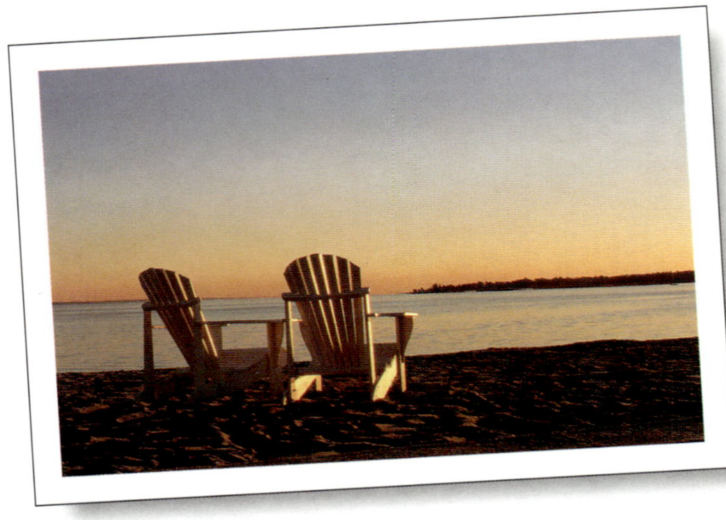

▲ **EMBELLISHING YOUR SUBJECT** My photo didn't reproduce all the vibrant colors of the dramatic sunset I remembered. So instead of relying on the photo alone, I made small color sketches to get the feeling I wanted, and used a palette full of brilliant golds, bright oranges, and very cool blues.

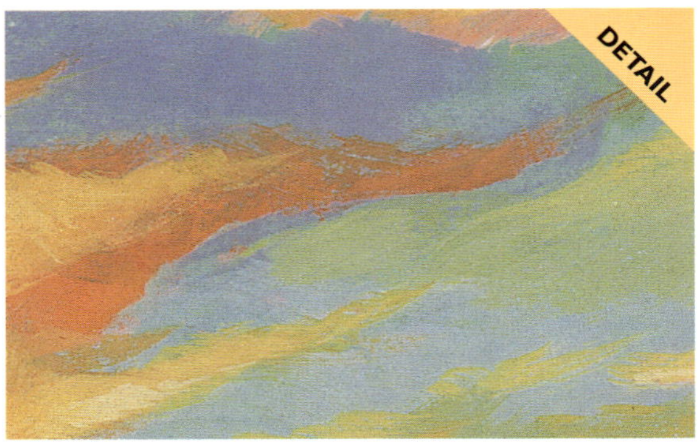

▲ **CLOUDS** I try to paint clouds with a sense of luminosity, as if the sunlight is filtering through from behind. In this picture, the sun is behind and below the clouds, so I use a very small brush and paint some sporadic highlights around the bottom edges. Then I add a bold yellow-orange edge to reflect the setting sun.

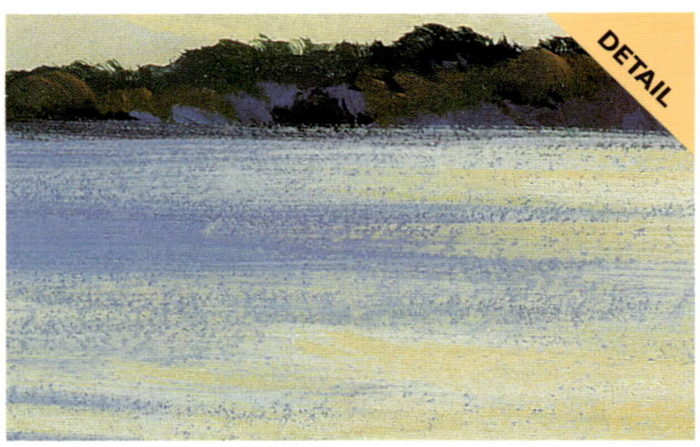

▲ **CALM WATERS** The ocean is much calmer in the late afternoon, so I keep my brushstrokes loose and lay them in horizontally to convey the subtle movement in the distance. I work some of my sky and cloud colors into the water for the reflections in the waves, making sure to keep the warmest colors close to the horizon.

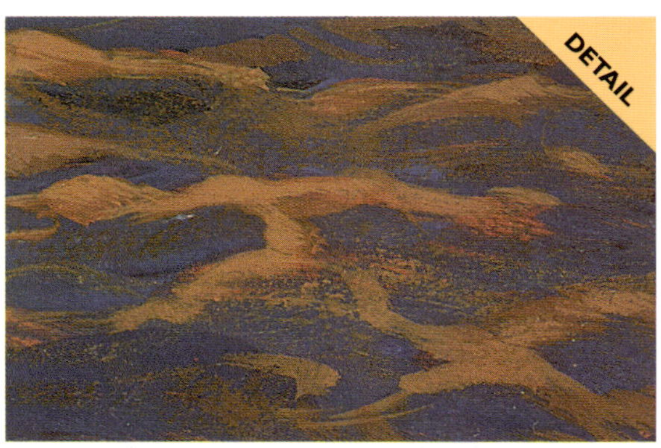

▲ **SAND** With a small round brush, I use a drybrush technique along the sand, dragging the brush across to create a rough, sandy texture.

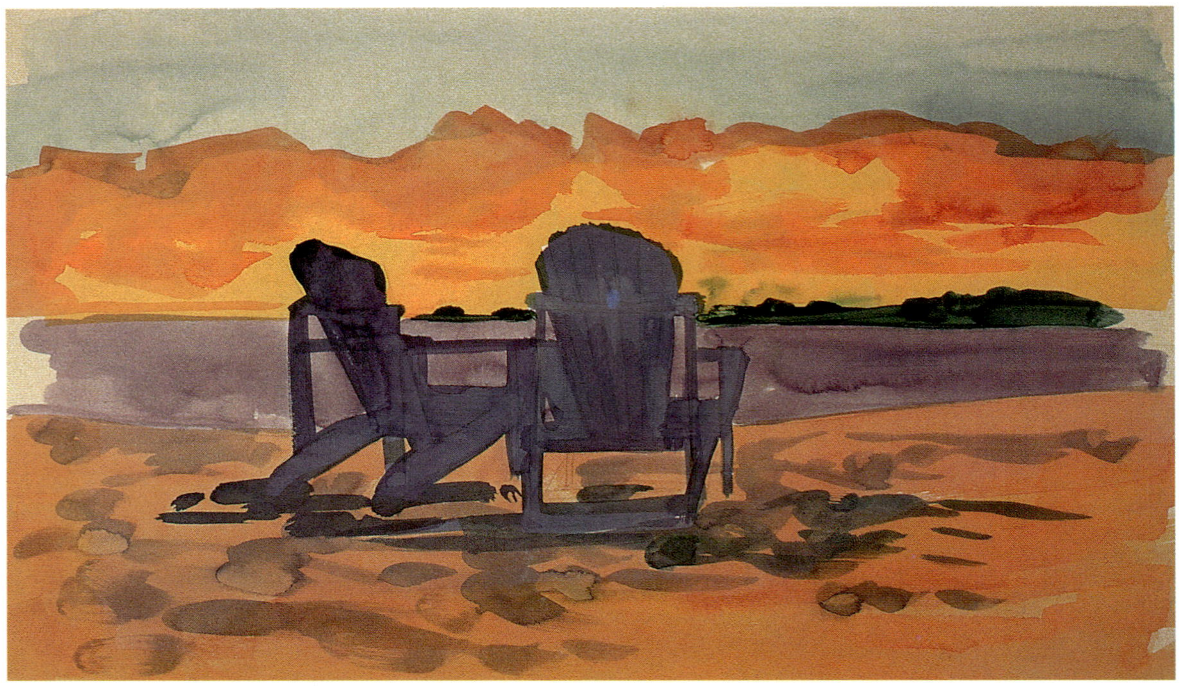

1 First I block in the basic shapes of the elements with washes of pure color. I use a small flat brush with phthalo blue to block in the chairs. Then I apply some preliminary sky colors, using yellows near the horizon and stroking in more greens and grays as I move up, away from the setting sun.

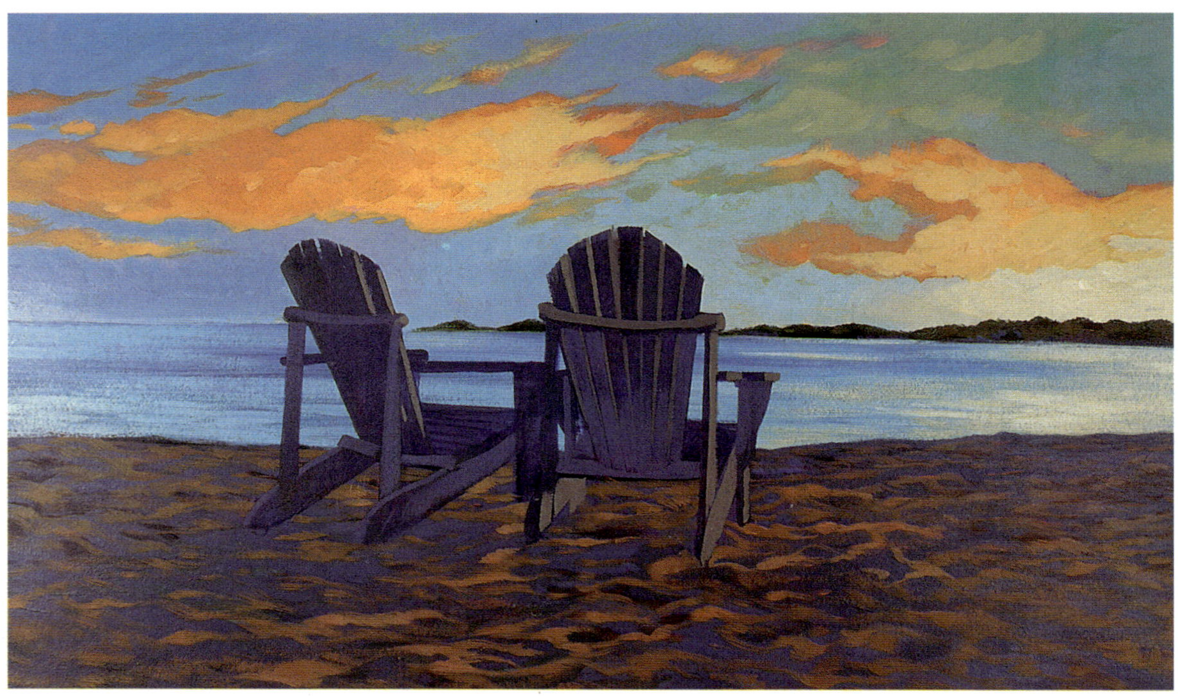

2 Working fresh, wet paint into the first layer of wet paint (referred to as *working wet into wet*), I quickly sketch in some indications of the clouds with a small filbert brush. I use the same brush and brilliant blue, ultramarine blue, and white with a bit of red for the sky and the shadows in the sand. Then I use my flat-edged brush and a mix of brilliant blue, acra violet, and a bit of burnt sienna to block in the chairs. I switch to a smaller flat brush for the sharp edges.

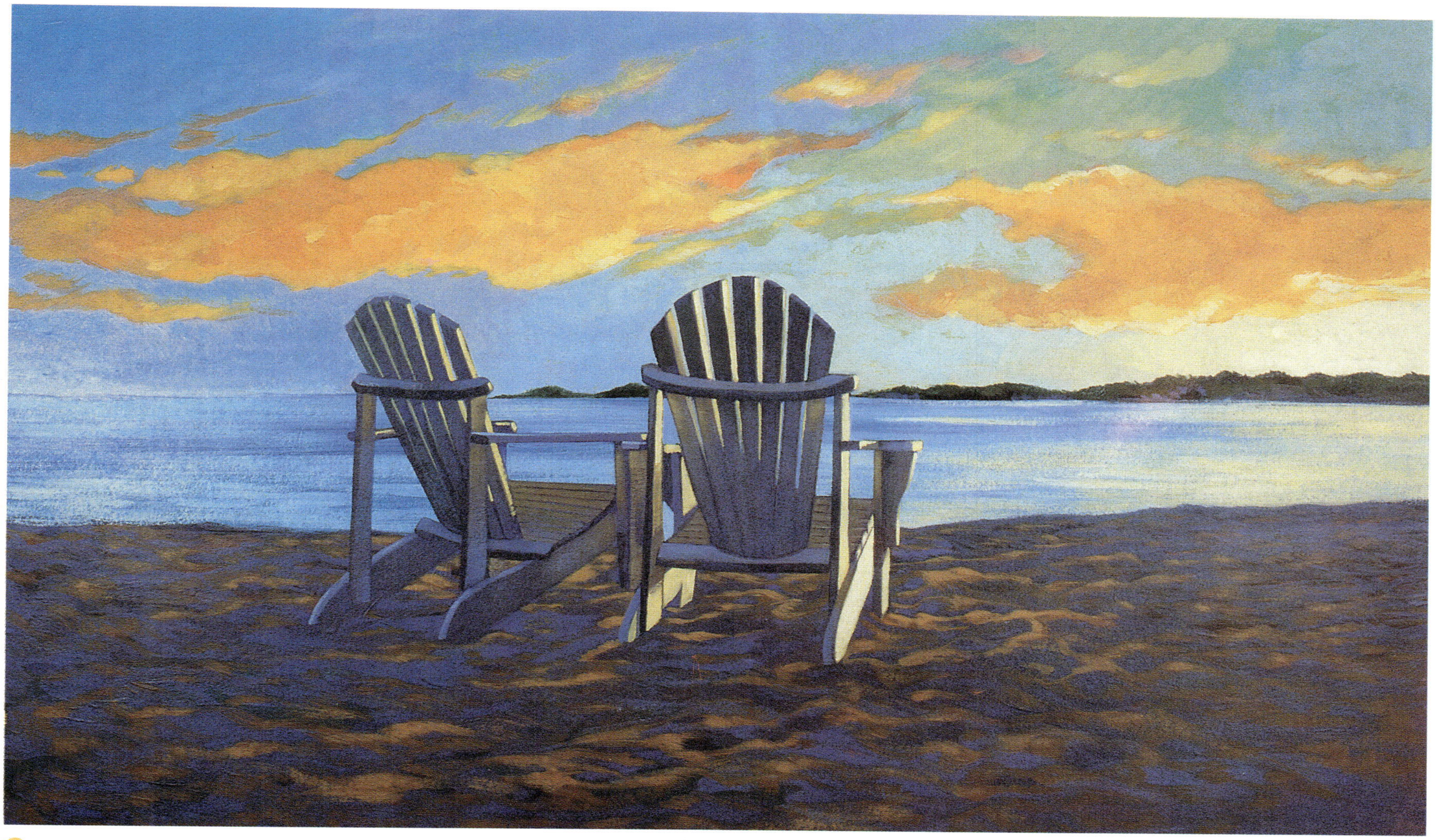

3 I establish the deep shadows with a mix of phthalo blue, acra violet, and turquoise green. In the sunlit areas, I add highlights of cadmium orange and white.

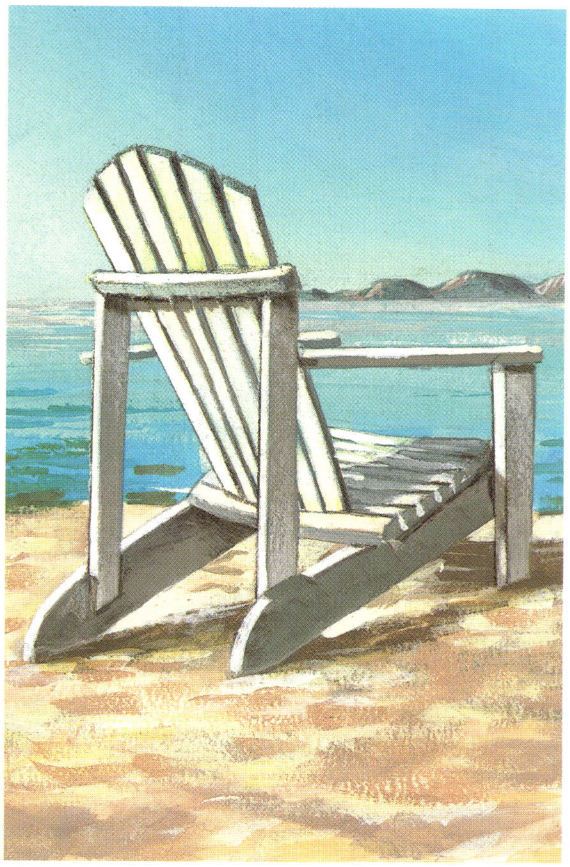

EARLY MORNING At this time of day, the colors are cool and crisp. The water is a mixture of light green and turquoise, and the shadows in the sand have a lavender hue. The sun is coming from low on the left, so there are warm highlights of bright yellow sunlight reflected on the back of the chair. The soft-edged shadows are slightly elongated and are cast directly in front of the chair.

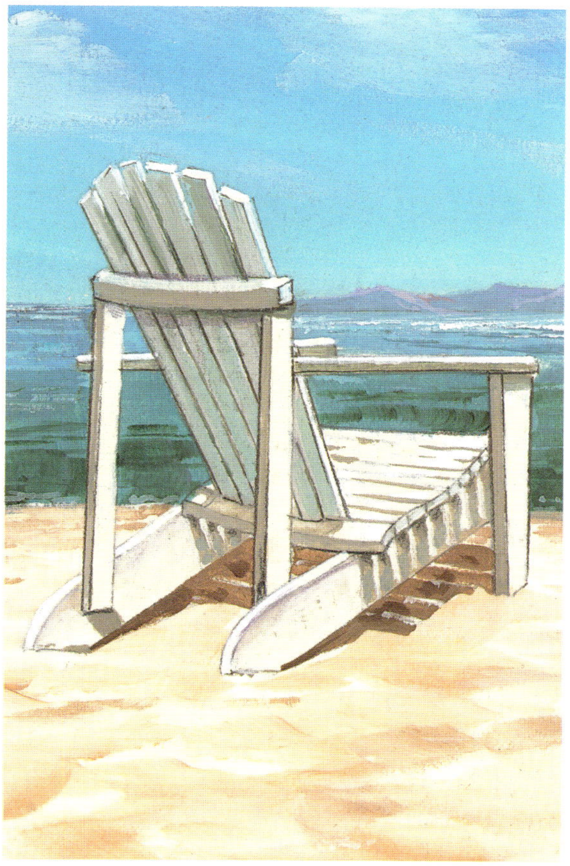

MID-DAY Now the sun is directly overhead, so the short shadows have sharp, hard edges and are almost directly underneath the chair. The back of the chair is no longer hit by the sun, so it is now in shadow. Overall the colors are more faded, and the ocean looks more active, with a greater range of colors. Here some light, almost transparent, clouds are visible in the sky.

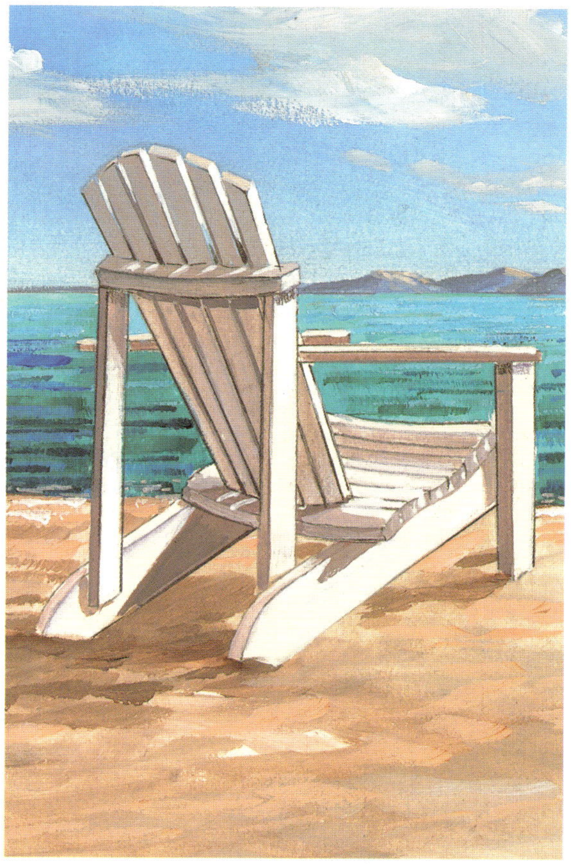

LATE AFTERNOON By this time, the sun has moved toward the right as sunset approaches, and the shadows are growing longer. Notice that the colors become much warmer, and even the white chair appears more golden. The deeper colors in the waves make the ocean appear calmer, and the clouds are beginning to stretch out across the sky.

Detail art by William F. Powell

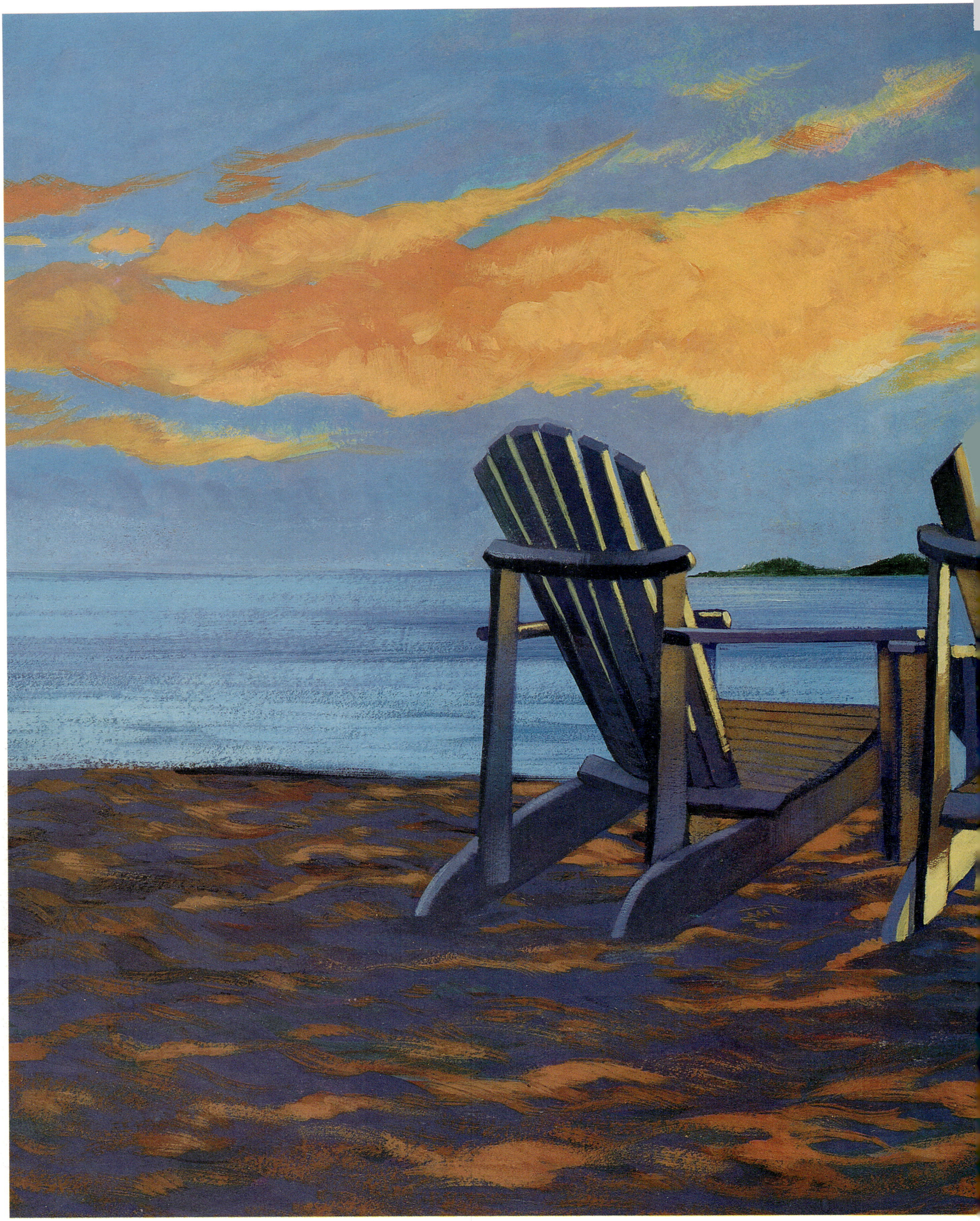

SEASIDE AT SUNSET Once I've added my brightest highlights, I'm pleased with the final result: a simple, tranquil sunset by the sea.

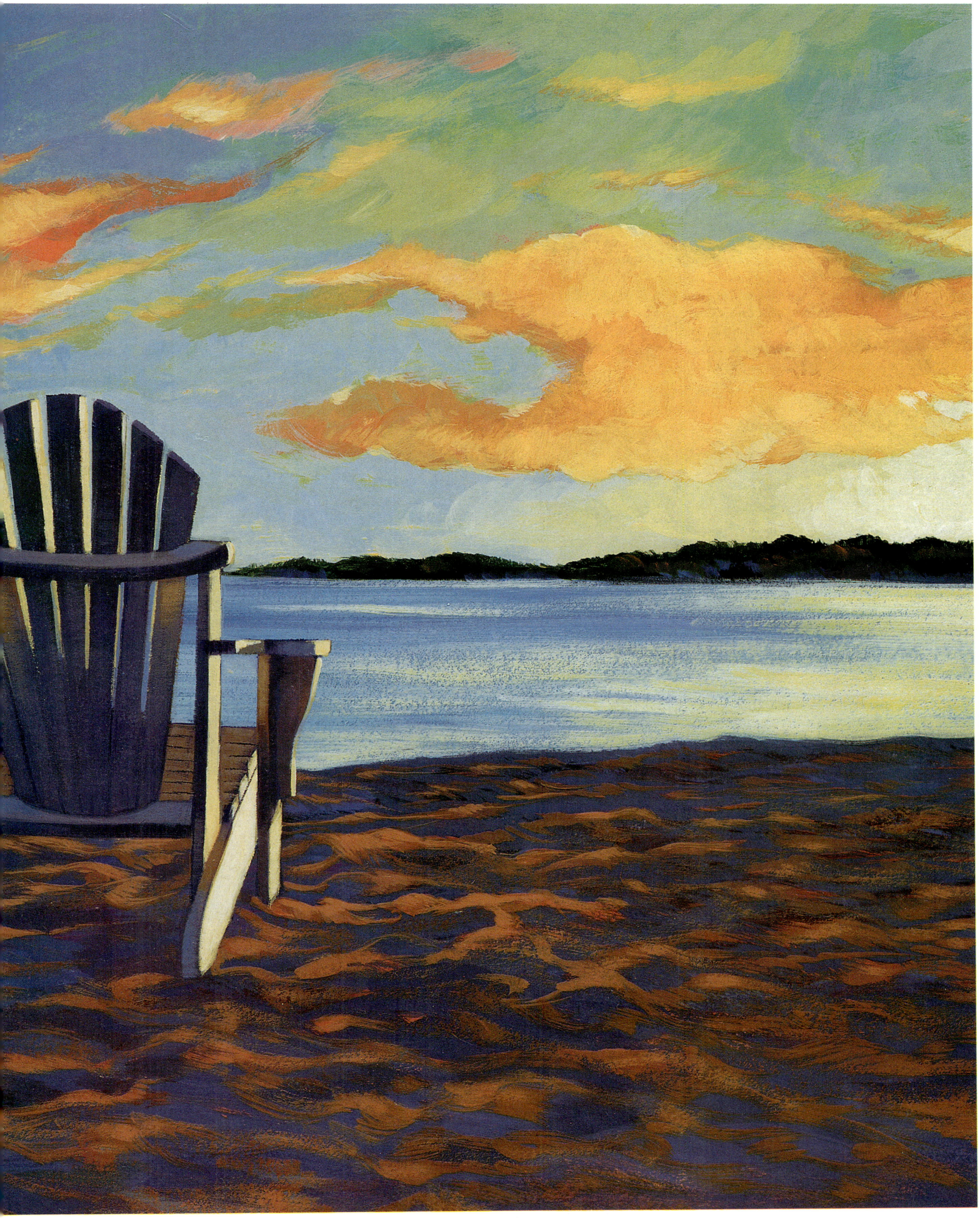

Creating Atmosphere

SOMETIMES THE MOST IMPORTANT thing about a particular scene is the feeling it evokes, rather than the subject itself. One of the most wonderful things about painting is being able to capture on canvas the atmosphere, or the mood I experience in a particular place and time. Then I can relive the moment every time I see the painting—and hopefully communicate those feelings to everyone who views it.

Conveying a Mood

The best way to express mood or atmosphere in a painting is through light and color. Light, bright colors convey a cheerful mood and bustling activity, whereas dark or muted colors seem more somber and quiet, as in this peaceful moment I captured of a deserted beach on a foggy day. The sky was dull and gray, so I focused on the nuances of color in the sand and the receding water, using neutral browns and grays and muted greens and blues to reflect the cool, damp weather. The mood was quiet but not depressing, as evidenced by the presence of one cheerful, bright blue boat.

CAPTURING THE MOMENT It was 5 o'clock on an overcast day when I was drawn to this scene—no time to break out my paints—so I snapped several photos at different angles and chose one to paint in my studio. I suggest that you keep a camera on hand, so you can quickly photograph any fleeting light or action that attracts you.

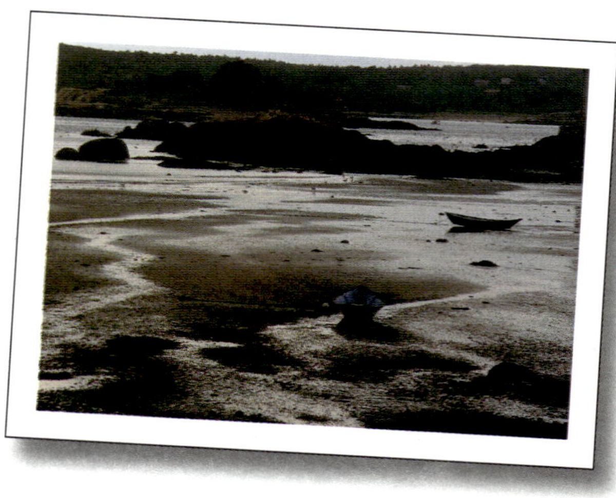

WORKING OUT THE SCENE I photographed this seascape both vertically and horizontally and then tried out a few sketches on drawing paper before committing myself to the board. I chose a horizontal format and toyed with the idea of showing more sky, but I wasn't happy with the empty expanse of gray. I finally decided to go with the view in the photo above.

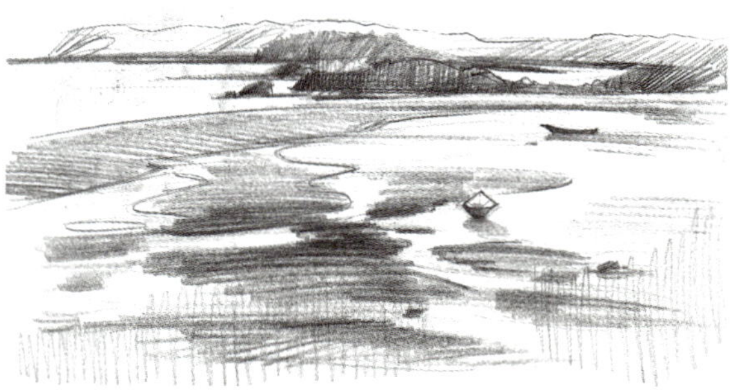

WATER MIXES

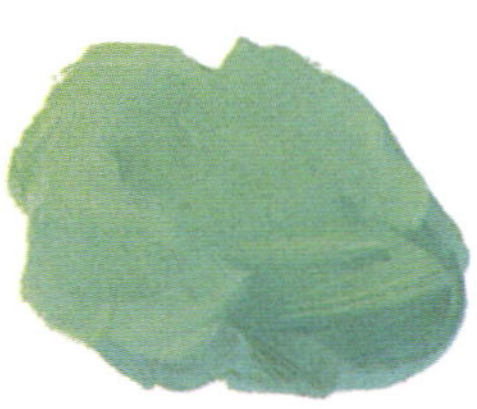

White, brilliant blue, and cadmium yellow

White, burnt sienna, and brilliant blue

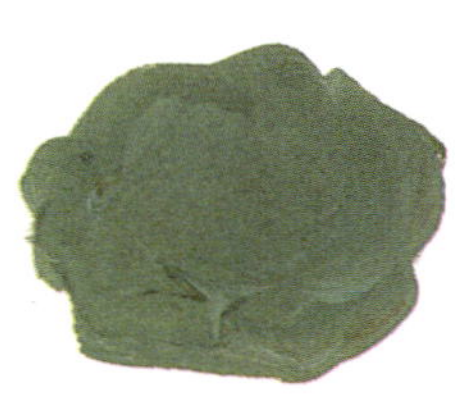

Burnt sienna, brilliant blue, and white

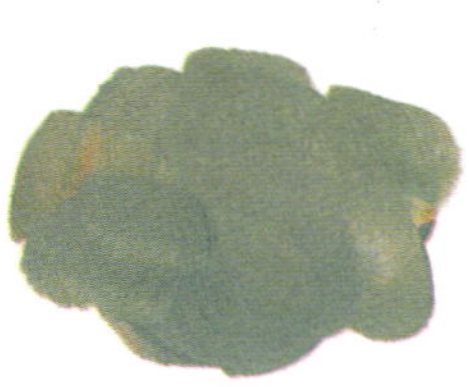

Burnt sienna, white, and phthalo blue

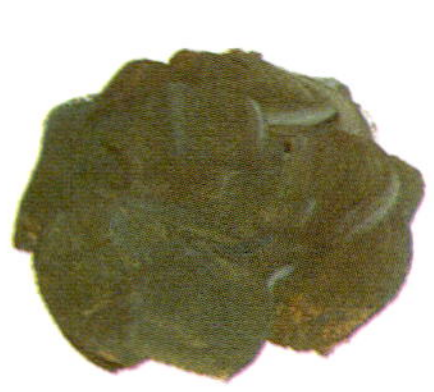

Burnt umber, white, and phthalo blue

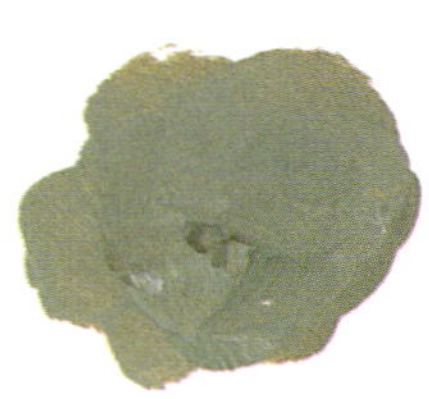

White, burnt umber, and phthalo blue

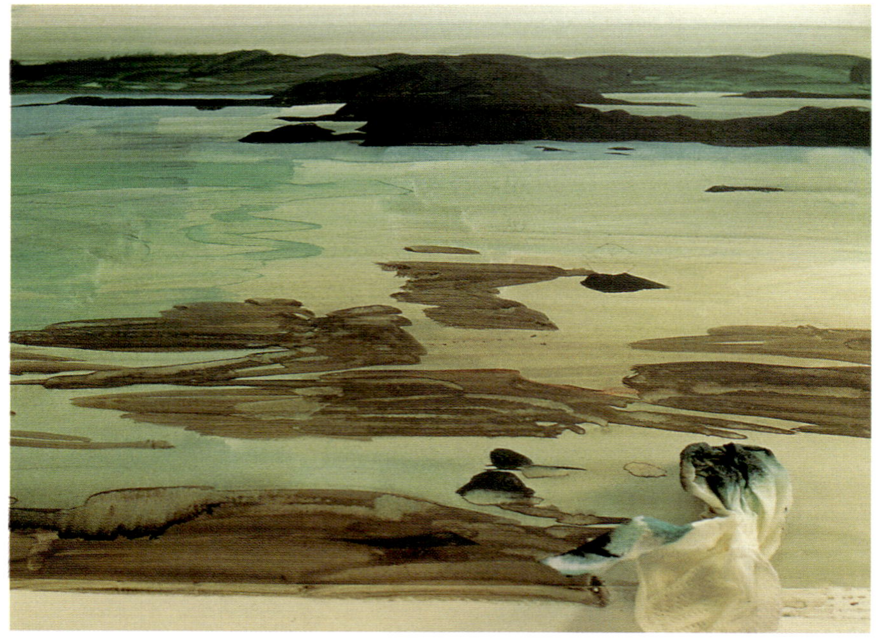

1 After sketching in my guidelines, I dilute mixes of grays and browns to a ratio of about 60% water to 40% paint. I lay in a wash of light brown with a large, flat brush and use a paper towel (see page 19) to wash in more haphazard patches of color. Then I add some subtle grays and blues in the background.

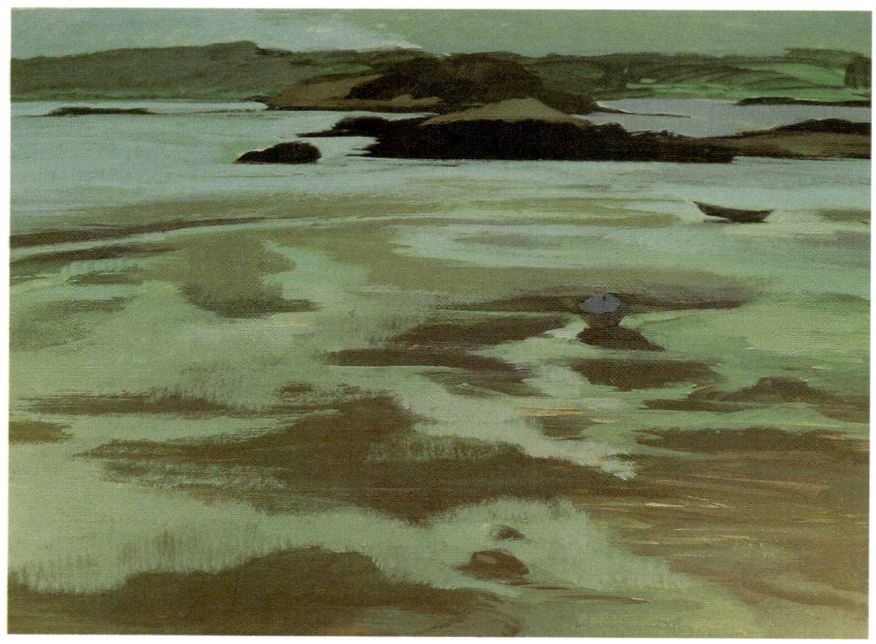

2 Light is important to any painting—even on a foggy day. My light source is in the upper left portion of the sky, so I brighten the water near that area with white. As I move farther away from the corner, I gradually add more and more blues and greens to the white. Then I use a dark blue to define the boat.

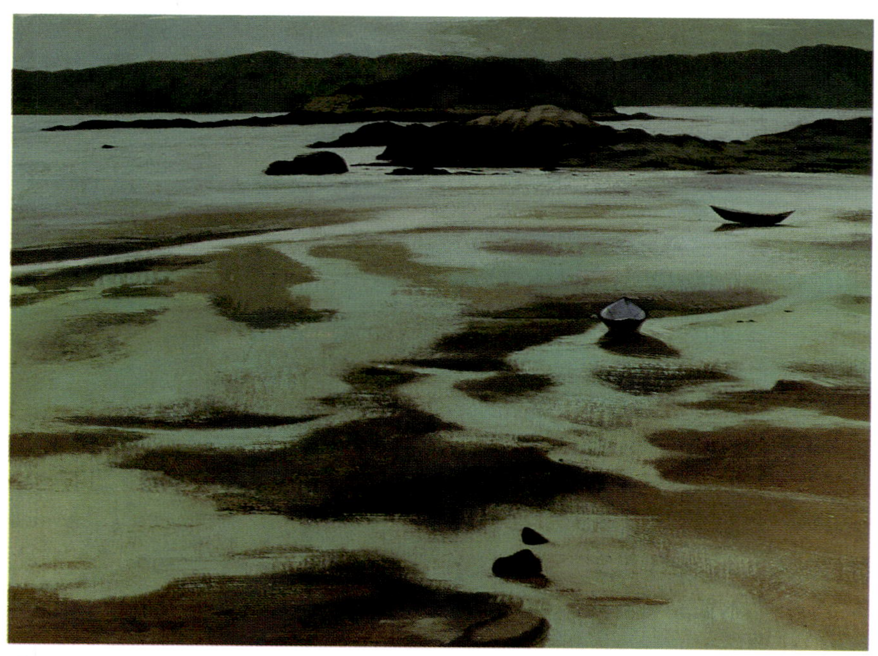

3 I begin to scrub in the darks with a bristle brush. This brush is great for painting in textured surfaces, and I especially like the way it brings the grainy sand and rocks to life. I switch to a small round brush to work in the smooth details of the boat with values of blue and a hint of white and turquoise green.

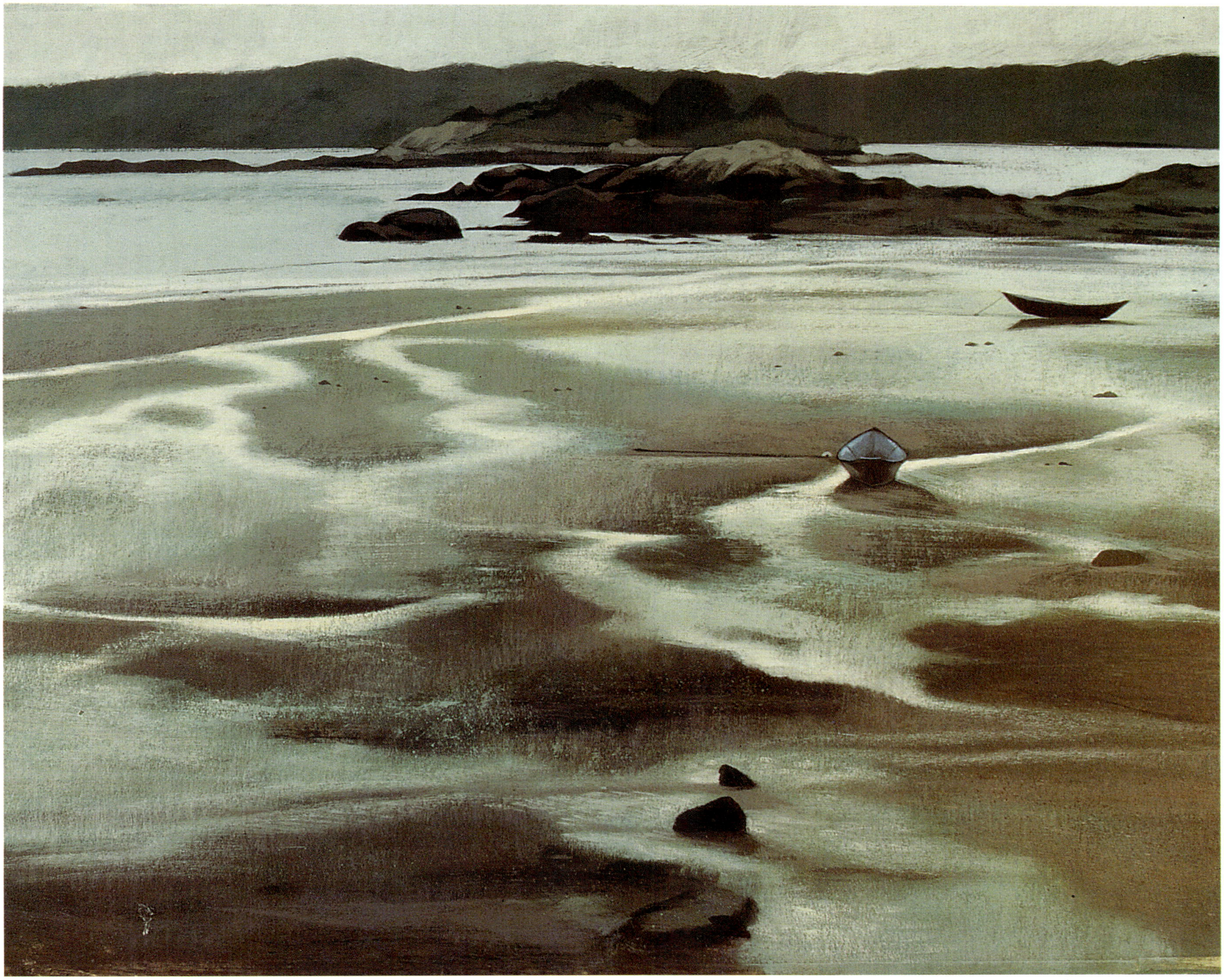

4 I add white and a touch of cadmium yellow light to boost the water channels. I stay true to my grayed palette, and I focus on the slivers of white water and the vivid blue boat.

Discovering Special Techniques

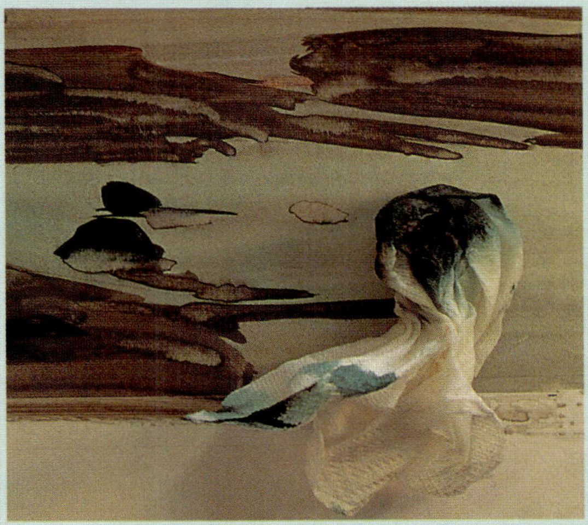

USING PAPER TOWELS A good-quality paper towel—that won't shred—is great for laying in washes. Dab the towel into the paint, and then drag and scrub across the board, letting the towel do the work.

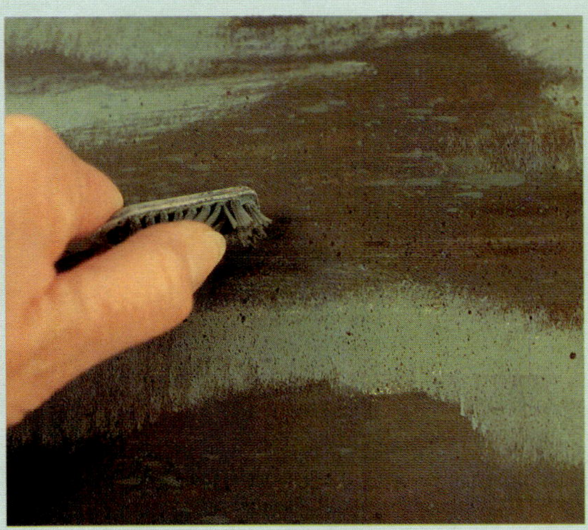

SPATTERING For the sand texture, create a 50/50 mix of water and color, and scrub an old toothbrush into it. Then run your finger across the bristles to splatter a fine mist of speckled paint across your painting.

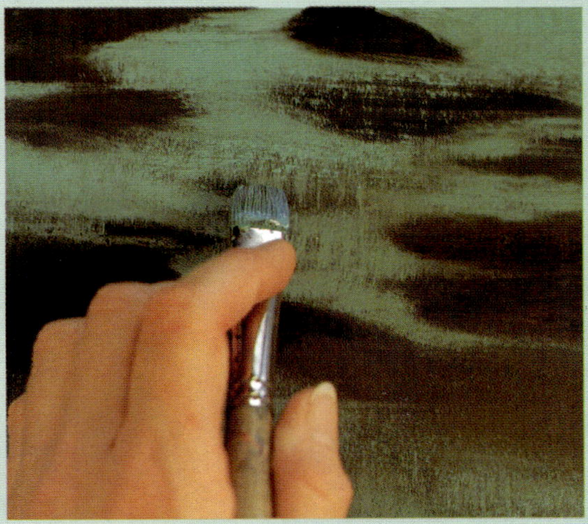

DRYBRUSHING Dip a stiff bristle brush in your paint and wipe off the excess so the brush is semi-dry. To add texture, vary the direction of your brush as you paint, dabbing vertically and stroking horizontally.

Using Transparent Techniques

ONE OF THE THINGS I LIKE MOST about acrylic is that I can vary the consistency of paint to suit my subject. I can paint with thick applications or I can use thin washes, much like watercolor—but acrylic paints have special qualities all their own. Unlike watercolor, acrylic colors aren't affected by water when dry, which means I can apply a wet color over a dry layer without muddying the color underneath (see the box on *glazing* on page 25). So with acrylic, I can paint thin, "watercolor-like" washes to achieve a translucent effect.

▶ WORKING WITH A VIEWFINDER To find a good composition outdoors, try looking through a viewfinder. Form a double "L" with your fingers or make a frame out of cardboard; then look at your scene through the opening. Try framing your subject from a variety of perspectives until you find a view that pleases you.

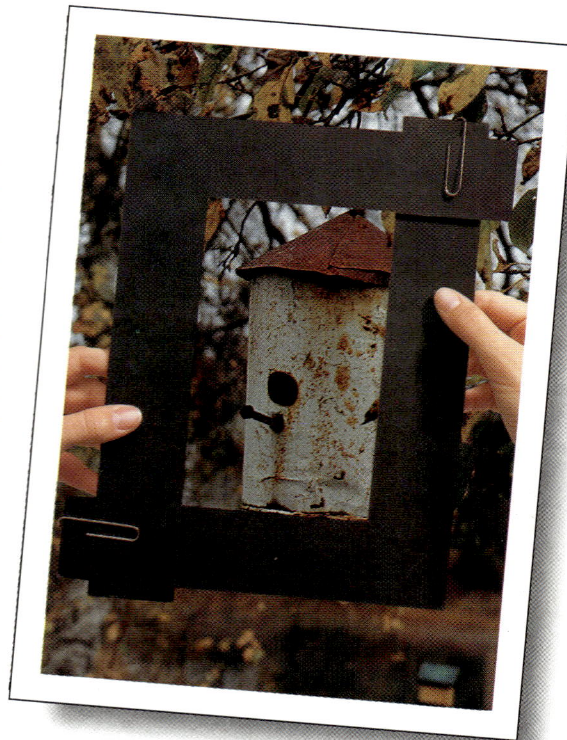

Washes of Color

When I use acrylic like watercolor, I build up my subject, wash by wash, as I did for this painting of a birdhouse. In a traditional watercolor manner, I start with light colors and gradually work up to my darks in layers, always keeping the washes thin and transparent. And with every wash, I look forward to "happy accidents"—those beautiful but unplanned effects caused when the water and paint react and start to run or drip on their own. It's these spontaneous special effects that add extra interest and character to my paintings.

1 I begin by scrubbing in a pale acra violet for the sky with a paper towel (see below). I leave the shape for the birdhouse within my phthalo blue and burnt umber background, but I don't have to save my white areas as I would with watercolor; instead, I can paint over my washes later with opaque paint. I use a medium flat brush to quickly wash in a variety of soft golden layers with raw sienna and a speck of turquoise green, keeping cooler colors in the distance and warmer ones in the foreground. Then I randomly block in some large leaves with a mix of yellow ochre and turquoise green.

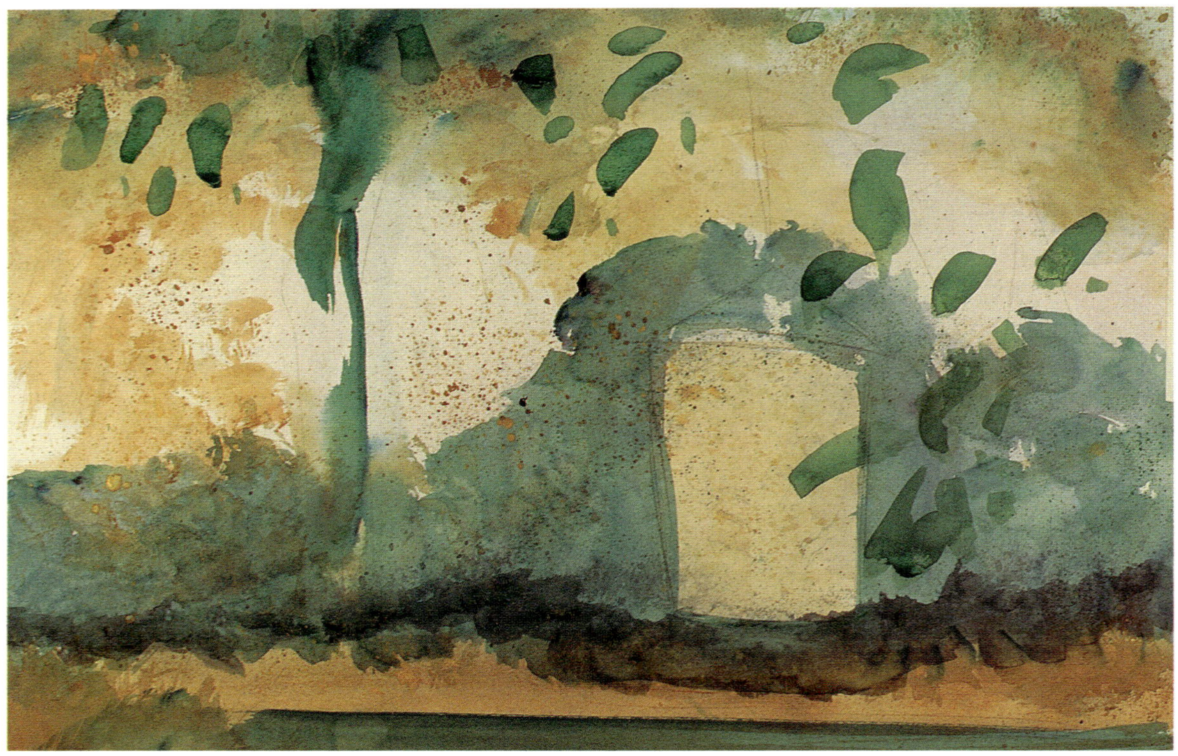

▶ APPLYING WASHES To quickly cover large areas with color, I loosely block in some of my shapes with a paper towel. I dilute the paint on my palette and then dab a damp paper towel into the paint. Then I drag and scrub the towel across my painting surface, creating a free and dynamic distribution of color.

2 Now I place in a few minimal details of the birdhouse—just so I don't lose its silhouette. I paint the rooftop with a mix of acra violet, burnt sienna, naphthol crimson, and white. I also stain some areas of the metal birdhouse with a rust-colored mix of burnt sienna and burnt umber. Next I drag in some blue-gray branches to the birch tree. For this middle ground area, I keep my paints diluted in a 50/50 ratio of water to pigment, using the same colors I used in step 1.

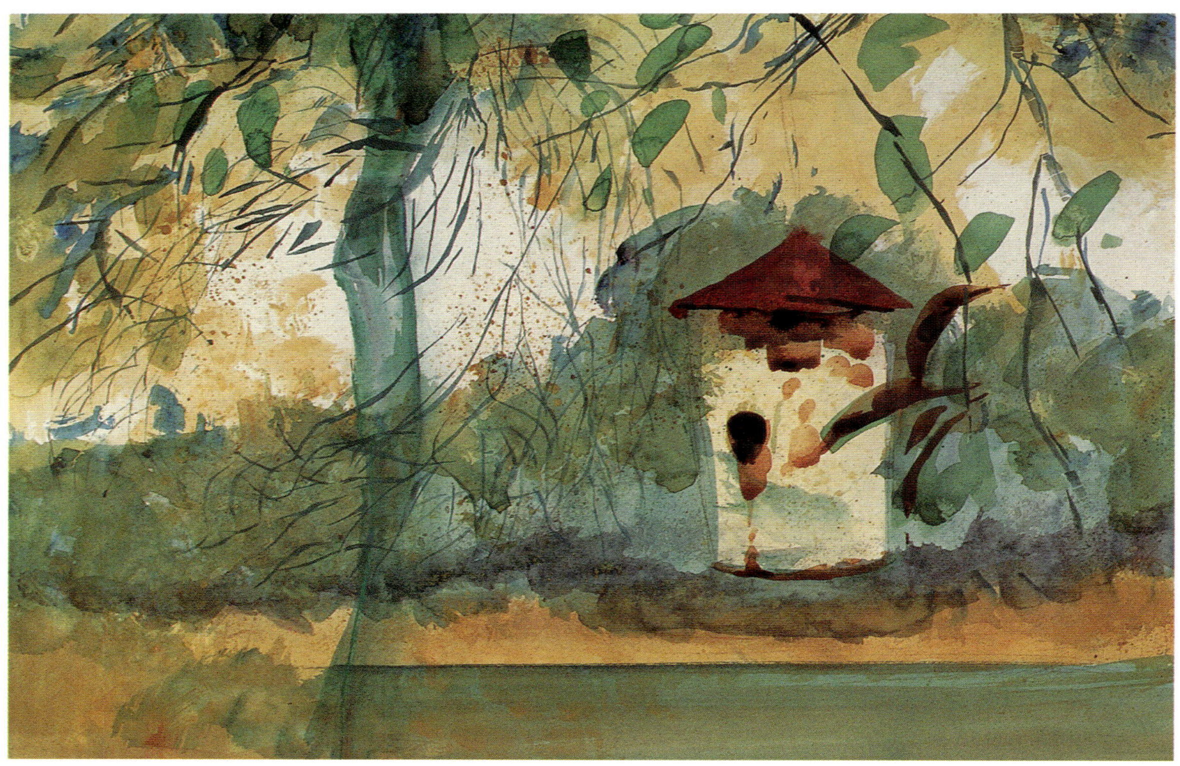

▶ PAINTING WITH STRIPS OF PAPER To create wispy textures for my grasses, I curl a 1-inch strip of stiff paper and dip it into diluted paint. Then I "stamp" the color onto the board, varying the placement of each blade to create a random pattern. Where I want the texture to pop forward, I add more pigment to the mix; where I want the grass to fade, I use more water.

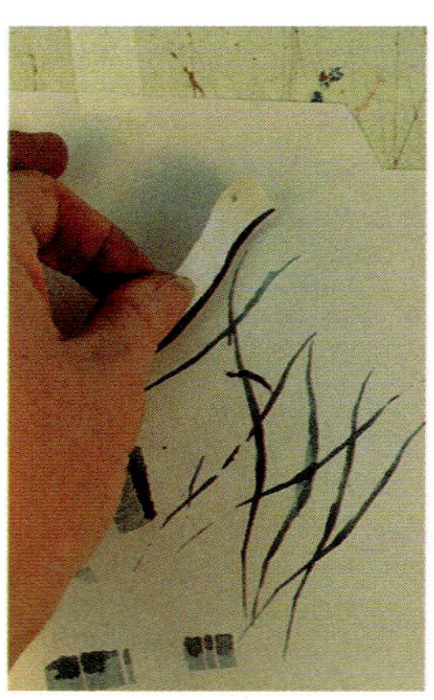

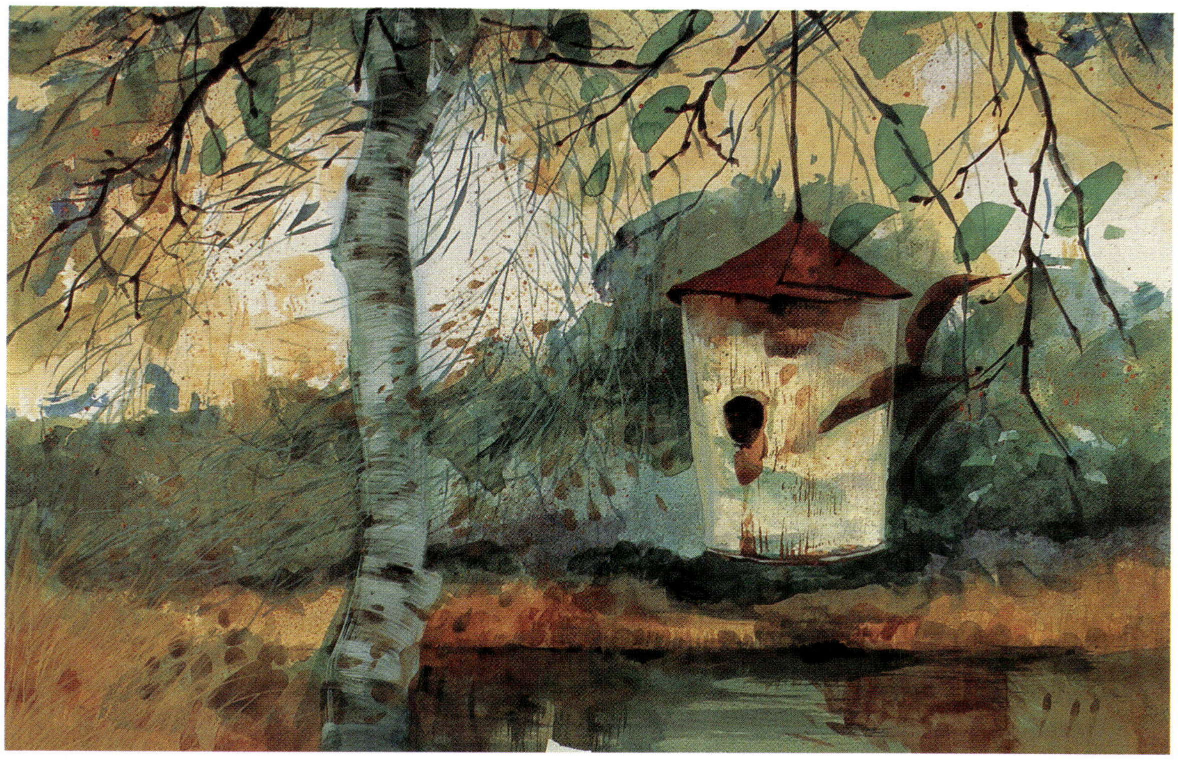

3 Using a small round brush, I place some branches in the foreground. Then I deepen the colors in some of the middle ground, concentrating on the area around the birdhouse so that it appears to advance forward. Next I switch to a large filbert brush and paint the large foreground leaves with mostly transparent mixes of turquoise green and yellow ochre, deepened with a bit of raw sienna. Then I top it with a more opaque mix of leaf colors.

Artist's Tip

Never let your brushes sit with acrylic paint on them. Keep them damp with a wet paper towel, and wash them periodically during a painting session to remove all the paint residue.

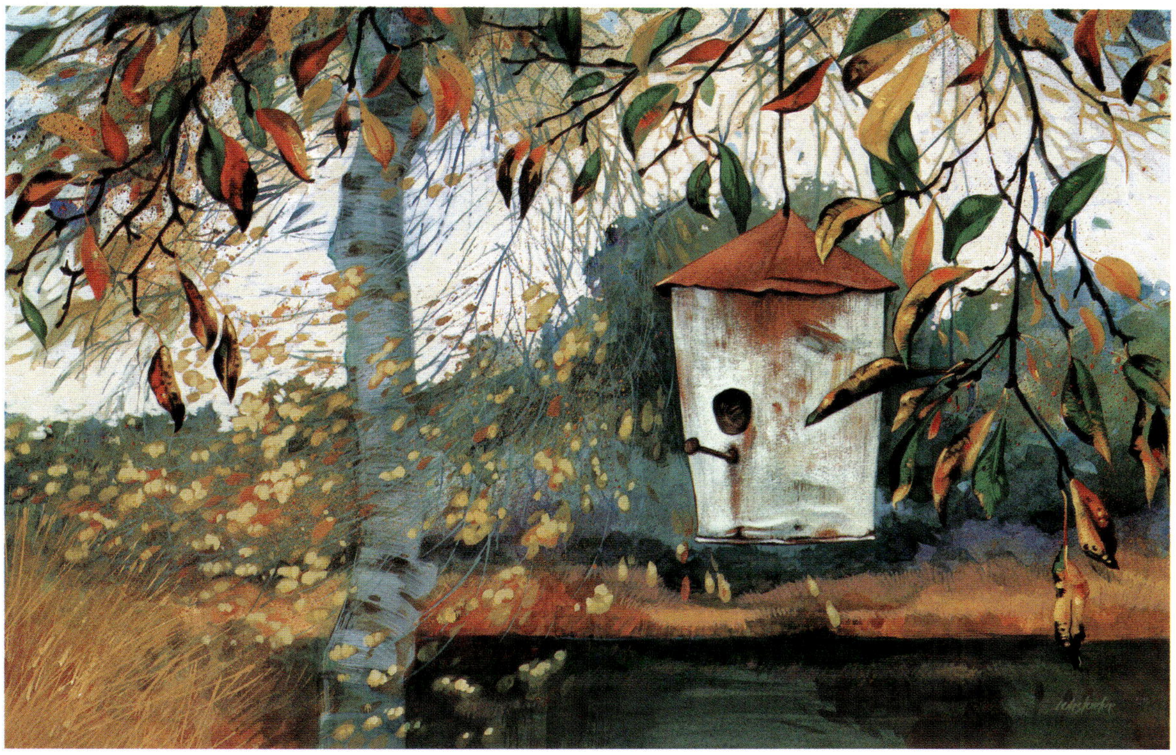

4 I finish my piece by adding details and textures. I soften the birdhouse with white and a speck of raw sienna and darken the roof with burnt umber and a little phthalo blue and acra violet. I add some depth to the pond and soften the reflection; then I add leaves and pods with mixes of white and yellow ochre, white and raw sienna, and spots of pure yellow ochre and raw sienna. Finally I add texture to the grasses with a few strokes of white and yellow ochre.

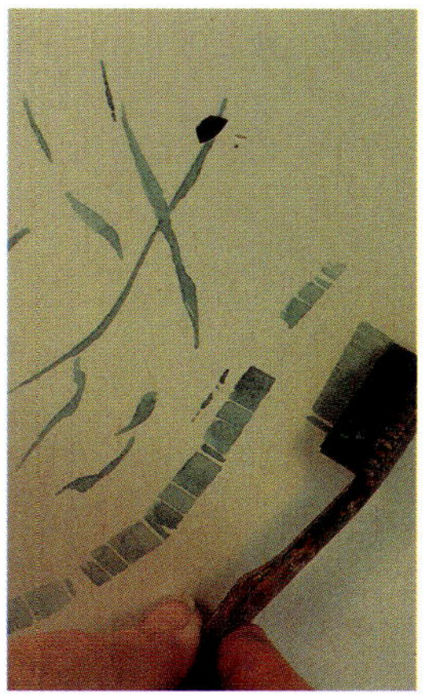

◀ **USING A TOOTHBRUSH** I love the texture I can get from an old toothbrush; it makes a perfect pattern for the birch bark—one that would be very difficult to duplicate with a paintbrush. Instead of dragging the toothbrush straight across the trunk, which would make it look flat and two-dimensional, I use the side of the toothbrush to make rounded strokes, following the curve of the trunk.

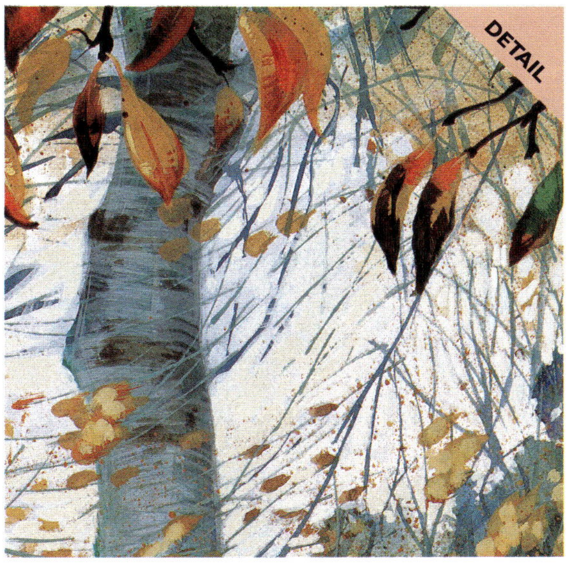

TREE BRANCHES To capture the likeness of these soft, wispy birch branches, I use the paper technique described on page 20. Here I use a mix of brilliant blue, turquoise green, white, and burnt sienna. I press the paper at random angles to make the branches look as if they are blowing in the wind; then I add the golden leaves with a very small round brush.

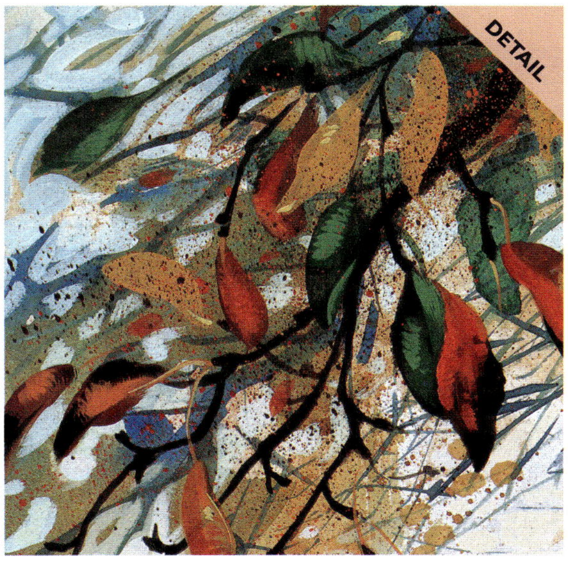

LEAVES I reserve the darkest colors for the branches in the foreground, to make them appear closer. To contrast with the light, transparent colors, I lay in the darks with an opaque mix of phthalo blue, burnt sienna, and phthalo green. For the tapering silhouettes of the leaves, I hold a small filbert brush loosely and turn it onto its tip as I make my strokes.

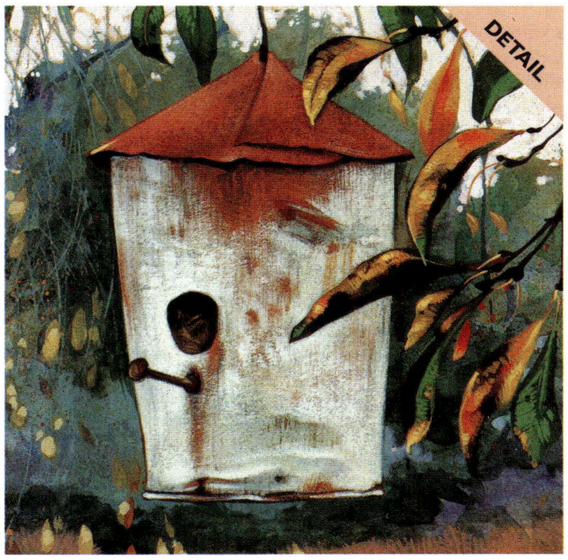

BIRDHOUSE I want the whites of the birdhouse to really stand out against the transparent colors of the background, so I mix opaque whites with tints of green, blue, and purple, just as I did for the sky. I use an old bristle brush to drybrush my whites onto the birdhouse, and then I add shadows and highlights to make it look dented and weathered.

Depicting Textures

NOTHING ENLIVENS A PAINTING as much as adding texture, whether it's the painted illusion of rough-grained wood or the physical texture created by thick applications of paint. And it's a lot of fun to combine the two in a painting! Because acrylic dries so quickly, it's simple to build up interesting layers of texture, and acrylic easily lends itself to a variety of texturing techniques.

Adding Realism to Your Painting

Not only do textures add interest, they also add to the realism of my piece, allowing me to imitate the look of rough bark, smooth glass, a sandy beach, or weathered wood, like the old siding on the house in the painting on these pages. Additives like painting mediums, sand, or sawdust can also help me imitate a variety of different surfaces. Adding plaster makes the paint look crumbly, like old whitewash, and adding crushed eggshells creates a look similar to rough stonework or sand. To create your own realistic textures, try the techniques I demonstrate on page 23, or just experiment on your own—it's all part of the joy of learning to paint!

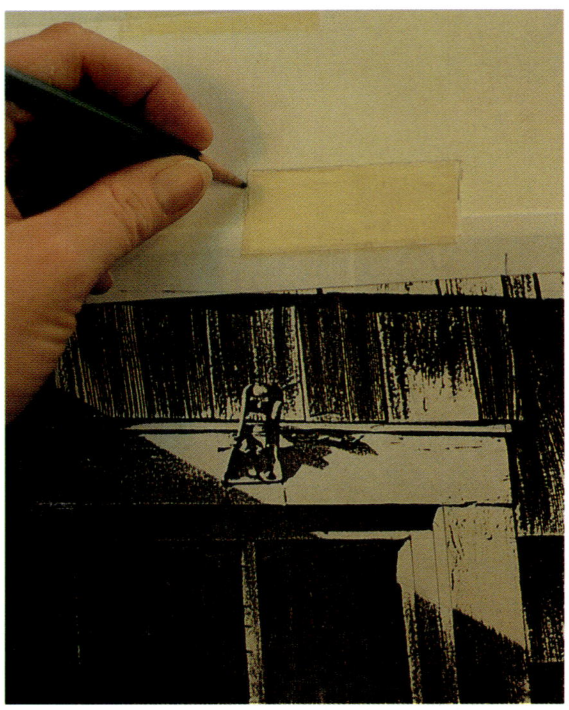

1 This window scene has a lot of straight lines and angles, so I decided not to try to draw it freehand on my board (and risk drawing the lines incorrectly!). Instead, I made an enlarged copy of my reference photo; then I placed a piece of transfer paper on my board (transfer paper has a carbon backing, similar to carbon paper), taped the photocopy on top, and traced over the lines.

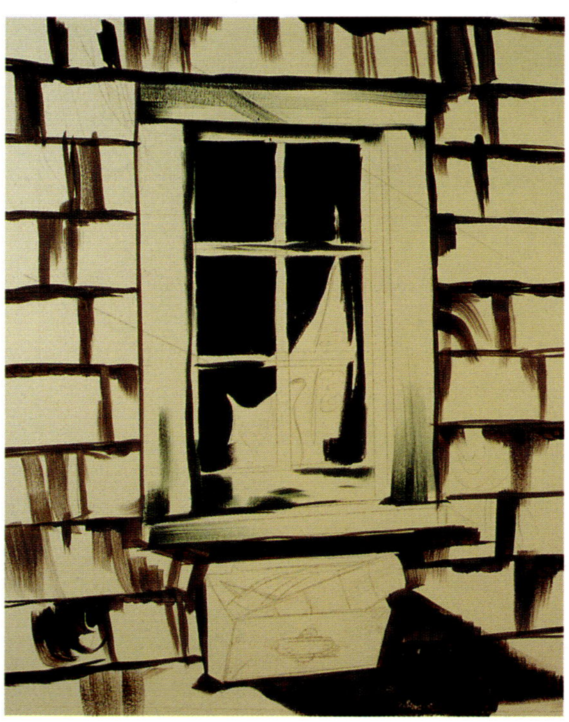

2 This painting is full of deep shadows, which define the shingles and architecture of the old house, so I begin my painting by establishing the darkest values first. For the dark areas behind the glass panes, I use a small flat brush and apply a black mixed from phthalo green, phthalo blue, acra violet, and burnt sienna. Next I wash in the outlines and dark shadows of the shingles, using neutral grays mixed from raw sienna, burnt sienna, and phthalo blue in a transparent 60/40 ratio of paint to water. I block in the shadows on the window frame with a slightly brighter color mix of turquoise and brilliant blue with a little bit of yellow ochre.

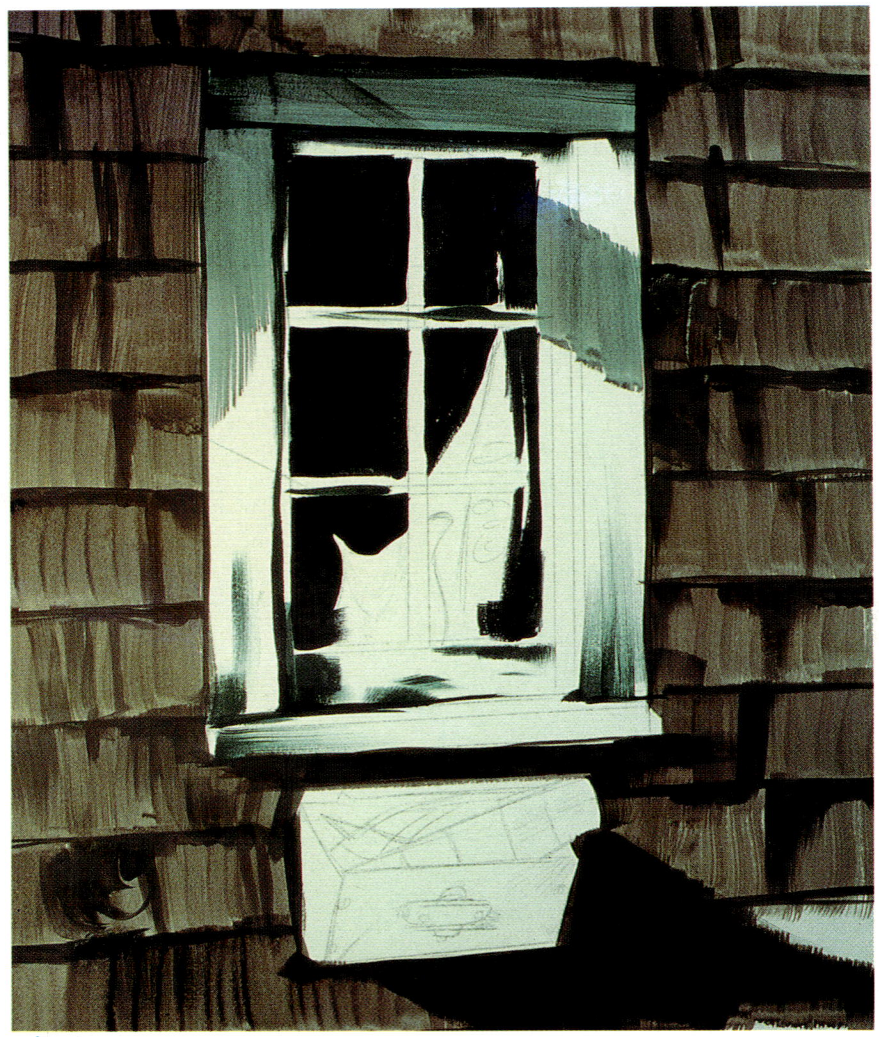

3 Now that I've washed in my first layer of transparent color, I continue building up my darks. I reinforce the blacks and enhance the deep shadows with a mixture of phthalo blue, burnt sienna, and raw umber. This gives me a base for achieving the maximum contrast between the darks and lights when I lay in the lighter tones.

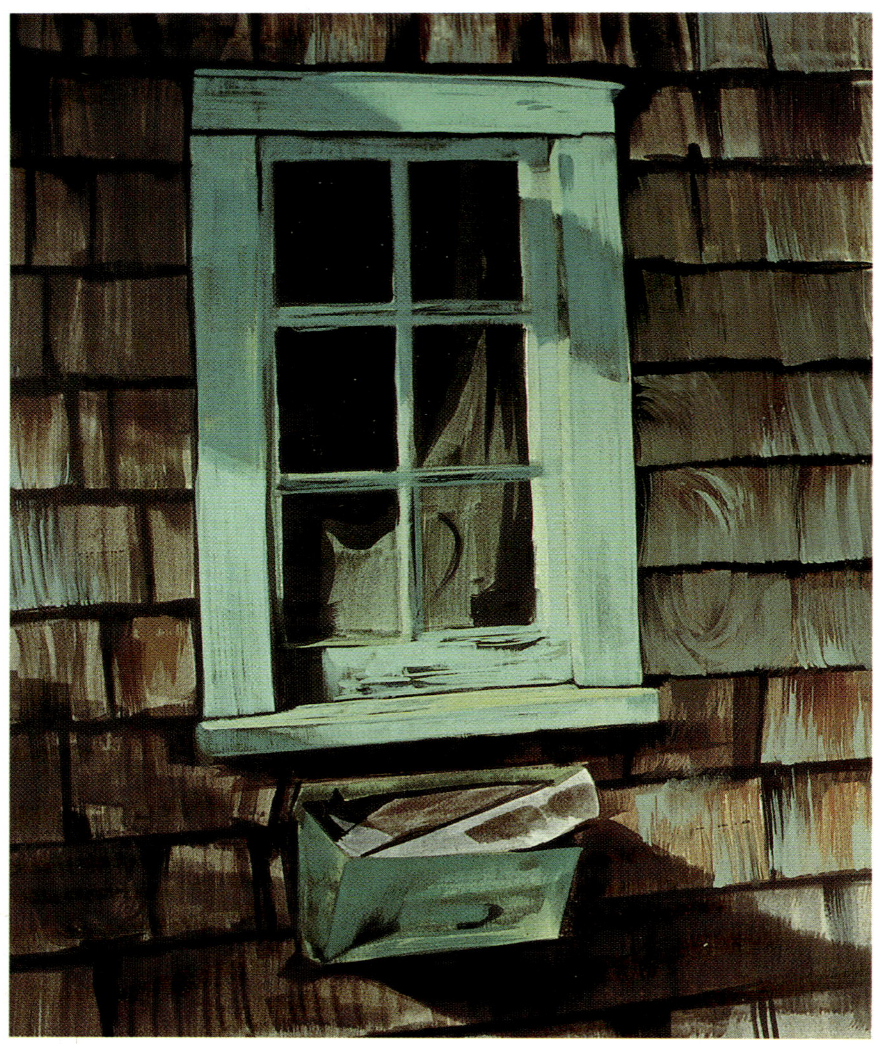

4 Still working from dark to light, I gradually add white to each progressive layer. I play with a multitude of neutral grays and greens, and I pay careful attention to the highlights. I add yellow to give warmth to the sunlit panes, pushing a cooler green in the shadows. Then, using a drybrush technique, I gradually build up the cast shadows.

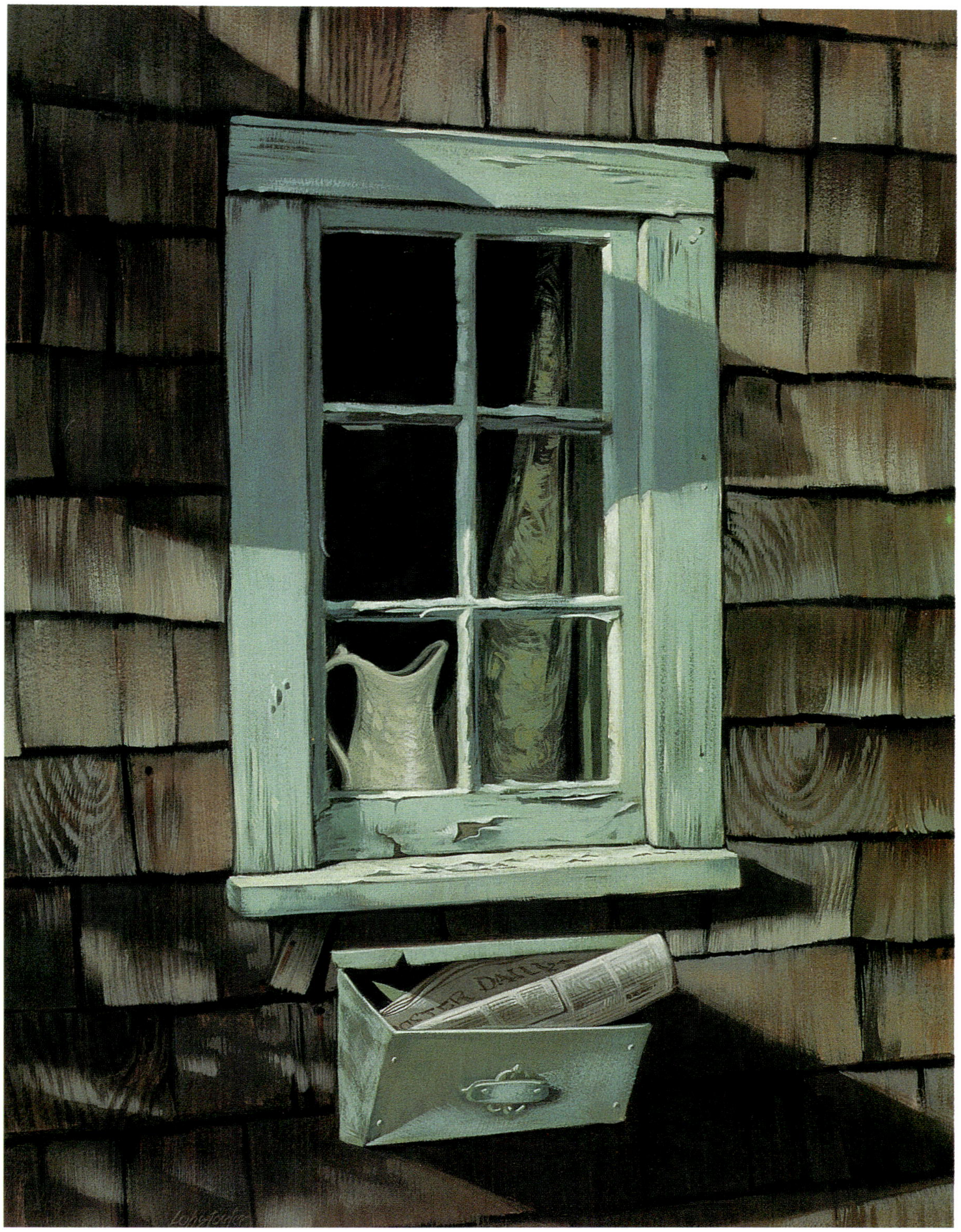

5 These old, weathered shingles require a subtle variety of warm and cool grays. And every shingle makes its own cast shadow, so I darken the shadow and highlight the bottom of each shingle. I drybrush the window frame with an old bristle brush to make it look more worn. Then I switch to a smaller round brush for the tiniest window details, and I go back over the chipped paint with a very small detail brush. When I stepped back to assess my painting, I decided to improve the composition by changing the position of the ceramic vase in the window; now the handle "disappears" behind the frame and the spout points in toward the curtain.

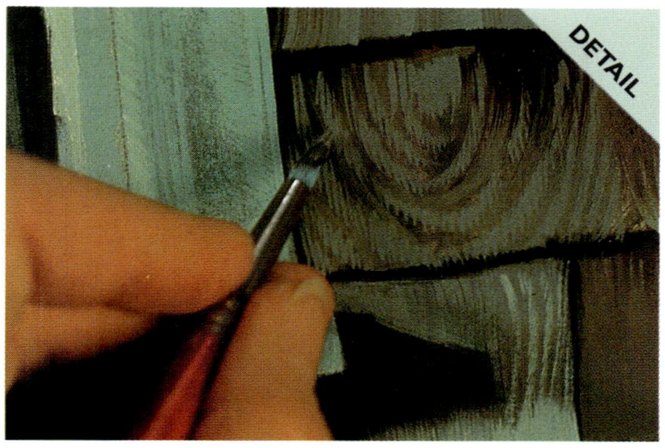

▲ **IMITATING WOOD GRAIN** I use an old, small brush with already frayed and separated bristles and load it with a small amount of opaque paint. Then I drybrush the shingles following the pattern of the wood grain.

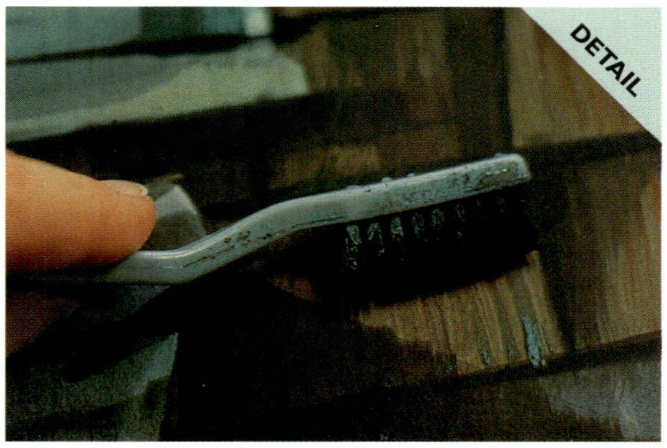

▲ **CREATING NATURAL TEXTURE** For the brittle, aged look of the shingles, I use the side of an old toothbrush. After I load the brush with an opaque mix of grays and browns, I place it at the bottom of each shingle and stroke the toothbrush upward.

Exploring Texturing Techniques

You've already learned that color advances or recedes in a picture depending on its "temperature," but did you know that thick paint will push itself forward more than thin, no matter what the color? You can create powerful three-dimensional effects by using thin paint for backgrounds and thick paint *(impasto)* for the forward details. Another advantage of thick paint is that it dries more slowly, allowing you to work into it longer. For simple textures, you can scratch patterns into the wet paint with a knife point or drag a comb through it. You can also build up interesting patterns by imprinting patterned objects into the still-wet surface. Or try mixing your paint with other substances, like sand or sawdust, to produce intriguing results. Whatever method you choose, try out various materials and patterns. Who knows where you may find inspiration?

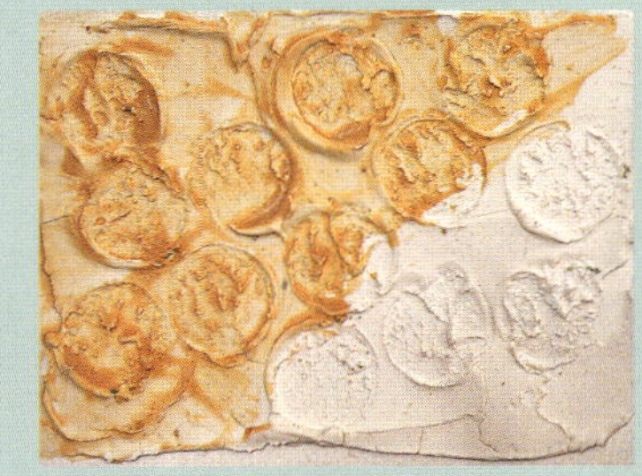

Press coins into modeling paste and paint them with a thin wash.

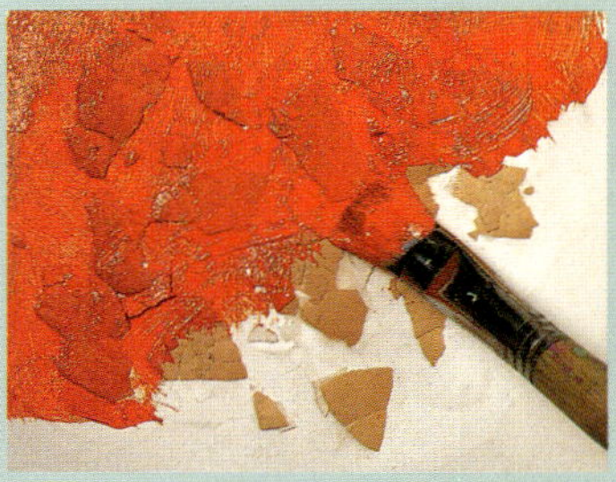

Adhere eggshells with gloss medium and paint over them with thick paint.

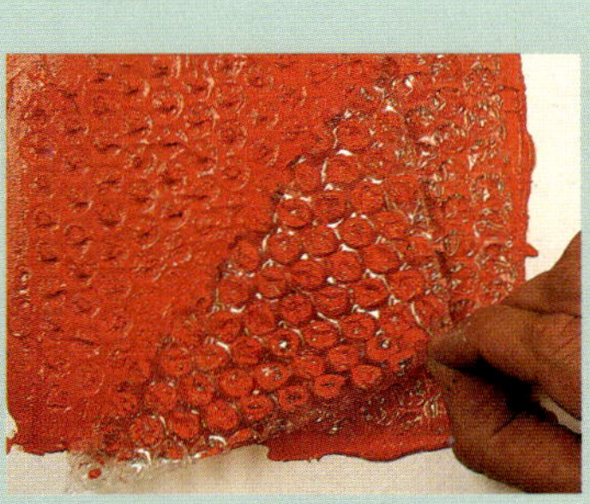

Press bubble wrap into thick paint to create an even texture.

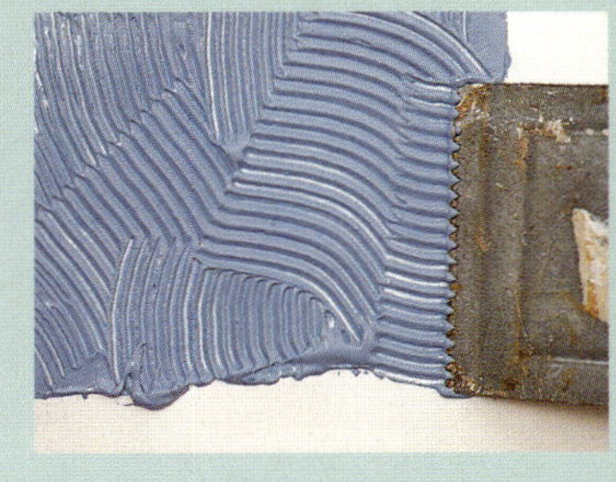

Comb or scratch into the wet acrylic to create simple patterns.

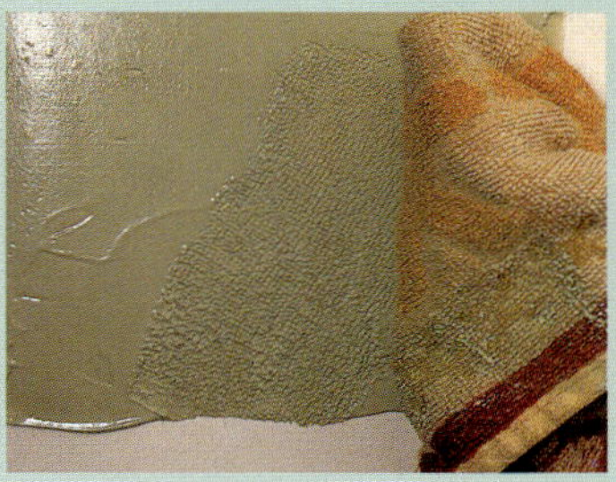

Press fabric into thick paint to produce a subtle texture.

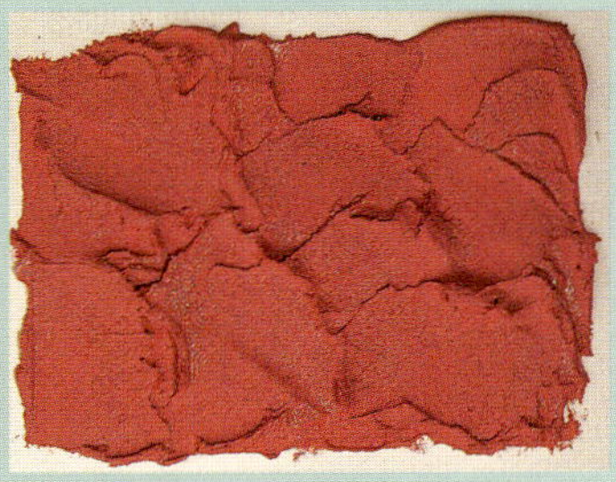

Mix sand into acrylic to imitate rough textures like brick or stone.

Painting Reflections

WATER ALWAYS MAKES an intriguing subject, even when it isn't the focal point of a painting. I like to add water to create instant drama and interest in a picture. Because water has the qualities of both a transparent liquid and a mirror, painting it—and the varied colors and shapes it reflects—never ceases to be exciting and inspiring.

Rendering Reflections in Water

Water is very dynamic, with many shapes, forms, and depths. It can ripple and move with the wind, and its color depends on the colors of its surroundings. There are probably as many different ways to render water as there are forms it takes, but there are a few simple guidelines you can follow. When the water is still and glassy, like the lake in this shack painting, the reflections of the sky and other objects look like carbon copies. But moving water distorts the reflected images, rather than mirroring them precisely, so the reflections are elongated and their edges are blurred. But whichever type of water you paint, keep it simple—water doesn't have to be complex or fastidiously rendered to look realistic.

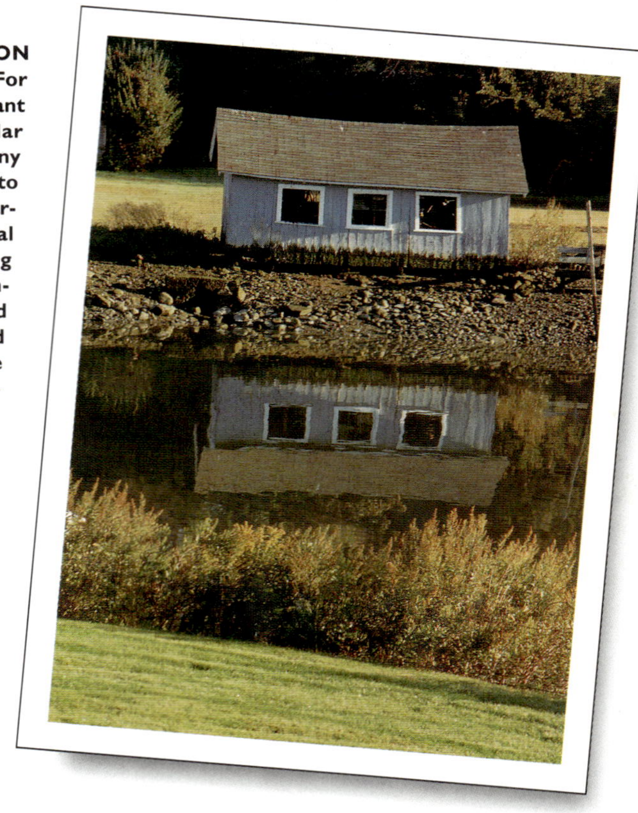

▶ FOCUSING ON THE DETAILS For this painting, I want to pay particular attention to any details of the photo that can add character to my final piece. The sagging roof, skewed windows, and crooked foundation all add to the unique charm of this lakeside shack.

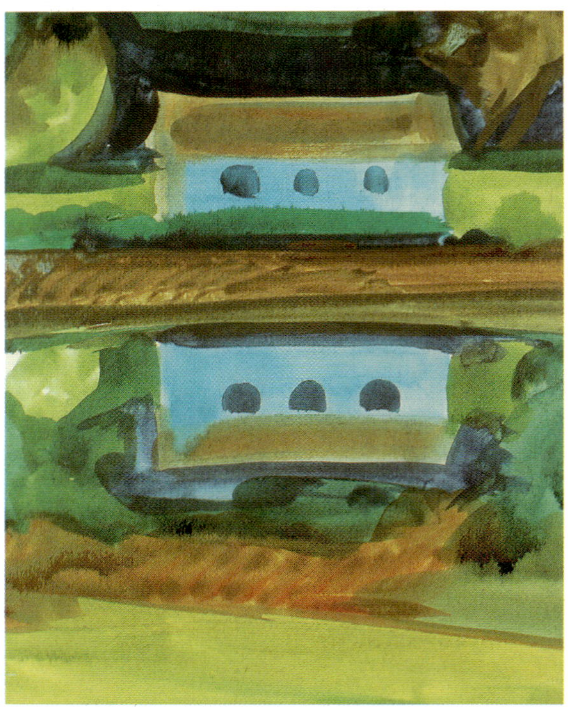

1 After drawing the scene on my board, I paint my first layer of washes in pure, bright colors, without adding any white. Then I redefine my original drawing with a graphite pencil, sketching over the details of the structure and the placement of all the elements. The lake water is very still, so I take particular care when I draw the reflections, making sure they closely mirror the actual objects.

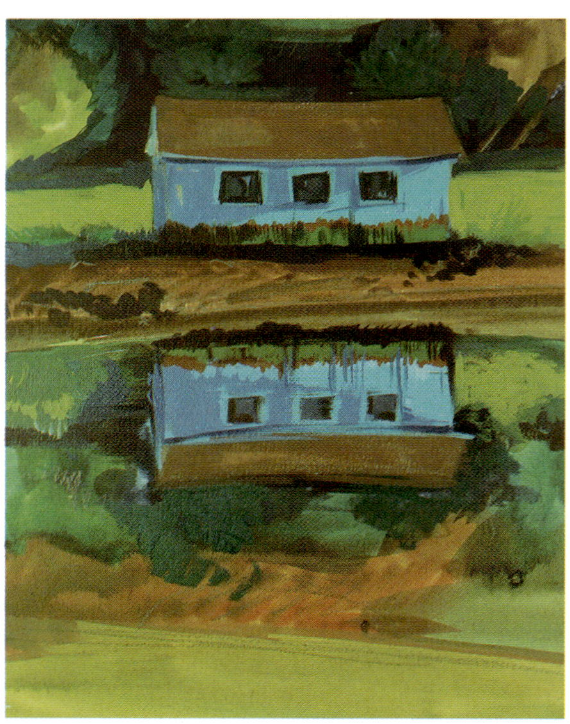

2 Next I begin building up the shack with broad brushstrokes, using turquoise green, white, brilliant blue, and a touch of cadmium yellow light. Turning the painting upside down helps me match the brushstrokes in the reflections. Working from dark to light, I use a small round brush to lay in the tree color with a deep, saturated mix of phthalo blue, phthalo green, acra violet, and naphthol crimson. For the smaller details, I switch to a very small round brush.

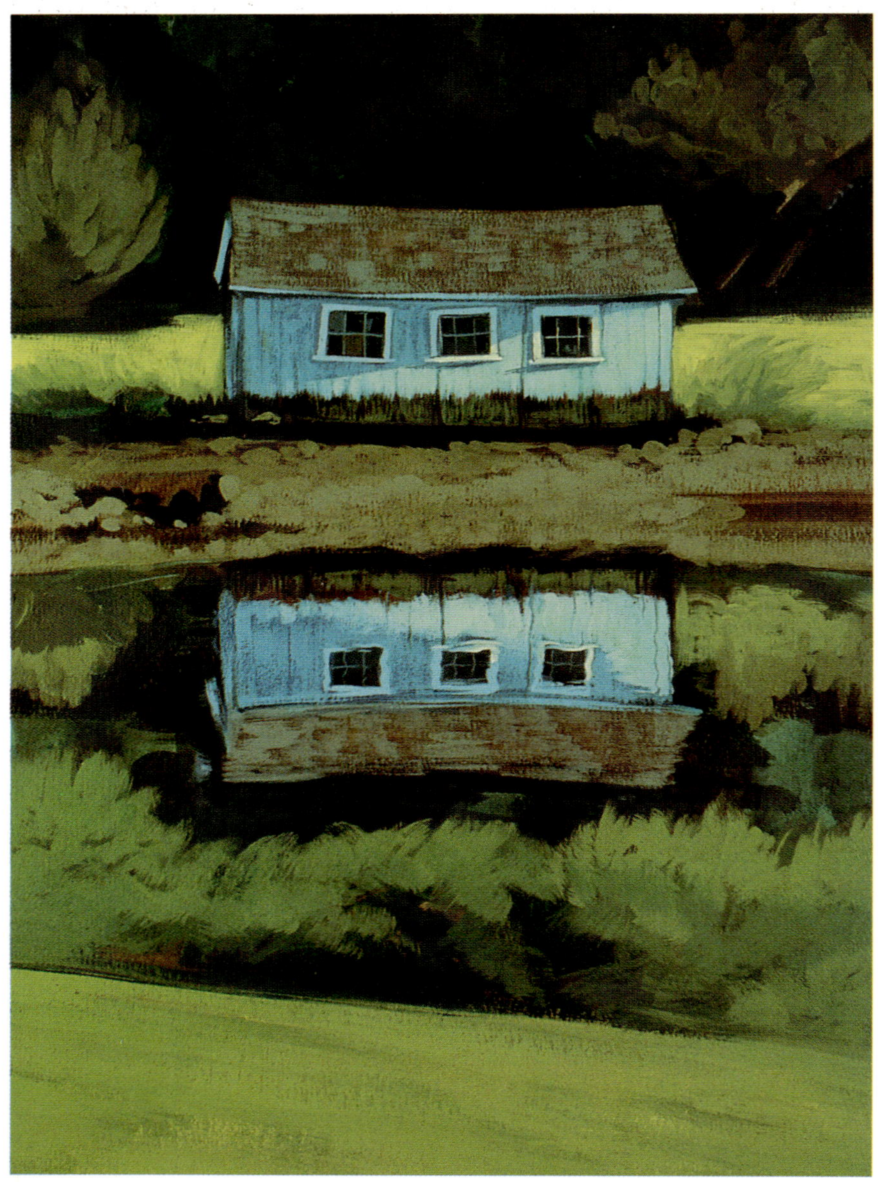

3 In this step, I try to match the color of the reflection in the water to the shack and its surroundings; in the next step, I'll differentiate the reflections with a glaze (see the box on page 25). I separate the real object from its reflection by changing the direction of my strokes. I paint the actual shack and the grounds with vertical strokes, but I pull the brush horizontally for the reflection in the water, wiggling the brush slightly in some areas for a ripple effect.

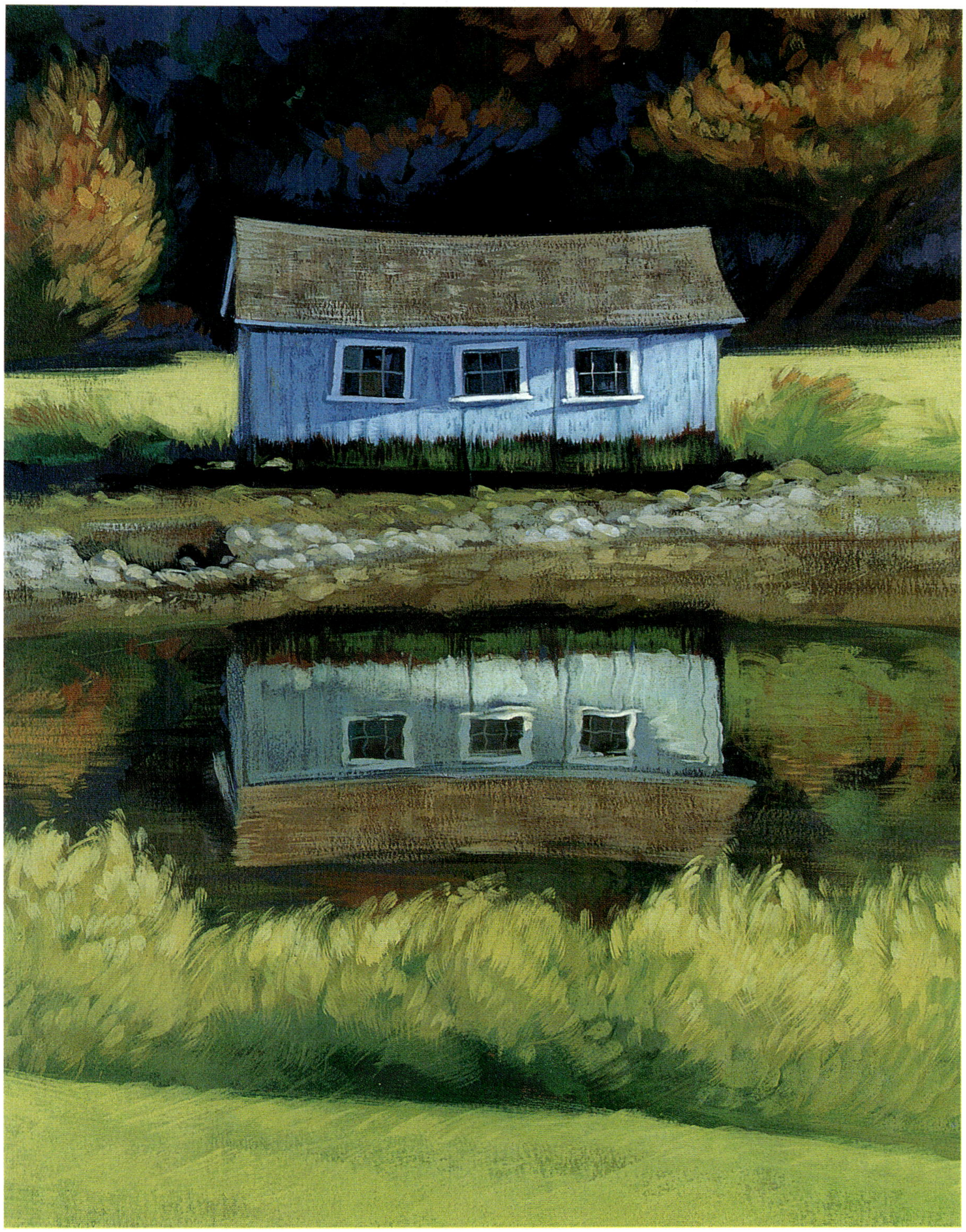

4 **After applying a glaze (see the box below) of yellow ochre and raw sienna with a touch of phthalo blue, I establish the foreground and add the final details. I boost the spots of sunlight by adding highlights of white mixed with a touch of cadmium yellow light. Then I use an old, frayed, flat brush to drybrush the side of the building, dragging the brush vertically to pull up some of the highlights. This creates an irregular surface texture, which makes the shack look weathered and aged.**

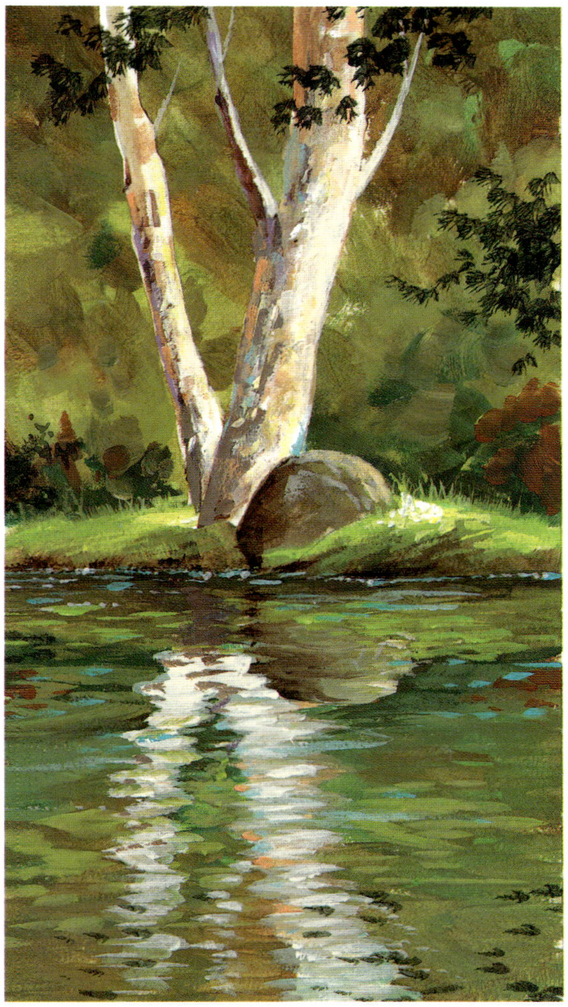

Art by William F. Powell

▲ CAPTURING REFLECTIONS IN MOVING WATER
To depict movement in the water, blur the edges of the reflections. If the water isn't moving too rapidly, limit the distortion to avoid showing too strong a current. As a finishing touch, add mottled dabs of color to indicate the pattern of light on the water's ripples.

Painting with Glazes

A *glaze* is a thin, diluted mix of transparent color painted over an existing color. Because the paint is transparent, each color shows through the one below, creating very rich color blends. You can use glazes to accent a base color; to create effects such as mist, smoke, snow, or sunlight; and to impart a sense of warmth or coolness, as shown in the example at right. Notice the difference between the unglazed corner (upper right) and the areas that have been glazed with warm yellow, strong red, and cool blue. For your glazes, start with about 95% water and only a touch of color. It's better to start with a glaze that's too weak than one that's overpowering; you can always add another layer when the first has dried. Then use a large, soft, flat brush and wash in a smooth layer of color with light strokes, carefully blending the edges of the wash into the background. Practice on scratch paper to get the feel of the technique before you apply it to a painting. I think you'll really enjoy all the interesting and atmospheric effects you can create.

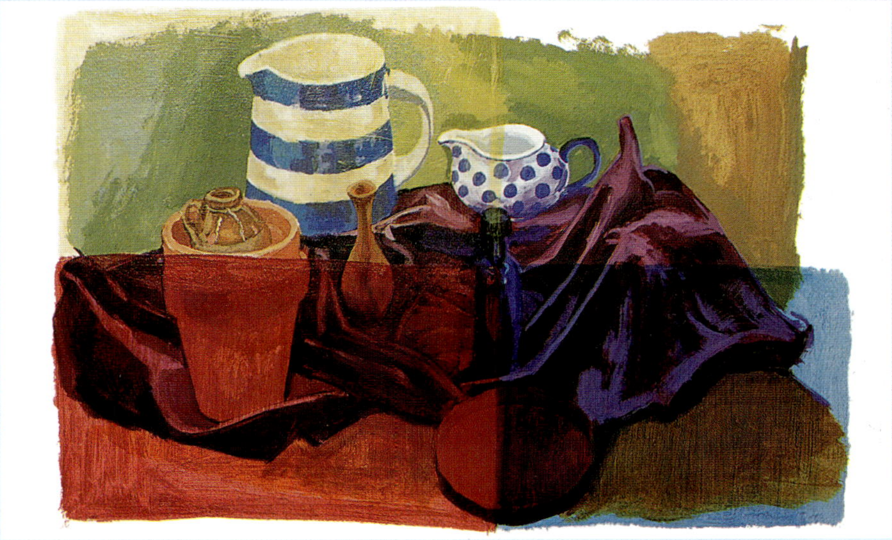

Portraying Depth

ONE OF THE MOST REWARDING THINGS about painting a landscape is being able to create the illusion of depth and distance on a two-dimensional support. It may seem challenging at first, but it is really quite easy. I just make sure I incorporate some of the visual cues used in landscape paintings to convey a sense of space and depth: size relationships, color variances, and atmospheric perspective.

Developing Distance

Atmospheric perspective refers to the fact that objects near us appear detailed and brightly colored, whereas they become hazy and duller in color the farther away they are. This is because dust and moisture in the atmosphere come between our eyes and the distant objects, making them seem bluer, grayer, and more vague. To create a sense of depth, I use the warmer, more vibrant colors for close objects and save the cooler, more subdued colors for those in the distance. Things also appear smaller as they recede, so I can suggest distance simply by painting near objects larger than those far away. In my painting of this doorway scene, you can see the three main levels of depth: the hills in the background, the houses and tree in the middle ground, and the shoes and doorway in the foreground.

▶ **MAKING ADJUSTMENTS** My original photo didn't show the detail of the upper doorjamb. But as I began to paint, I felt this composition needed enclosure, so I added that detail. I also decided to add color to the slippers and the tree. Making changes like this is called "taking artistic license." Once you feel comfortable with your medium, you'll feel more confident in taking your own artistic license.

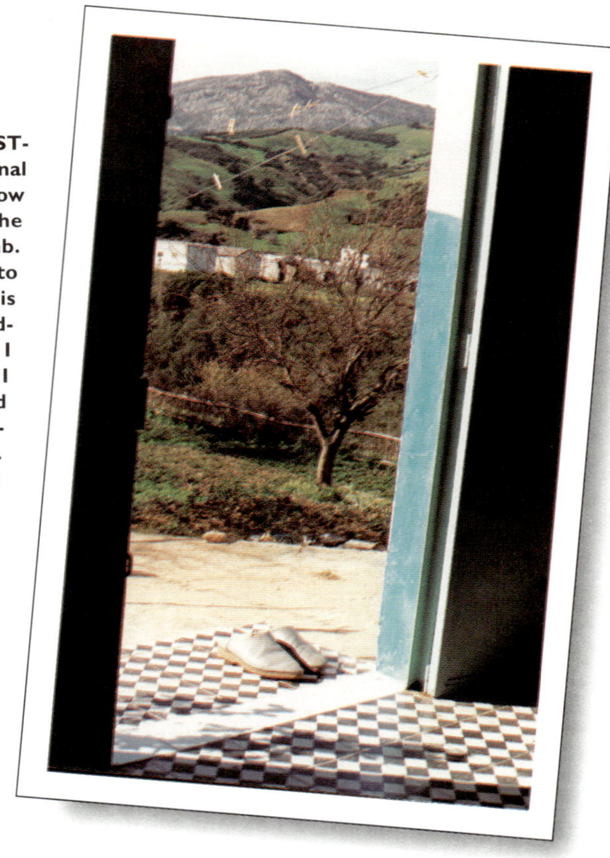

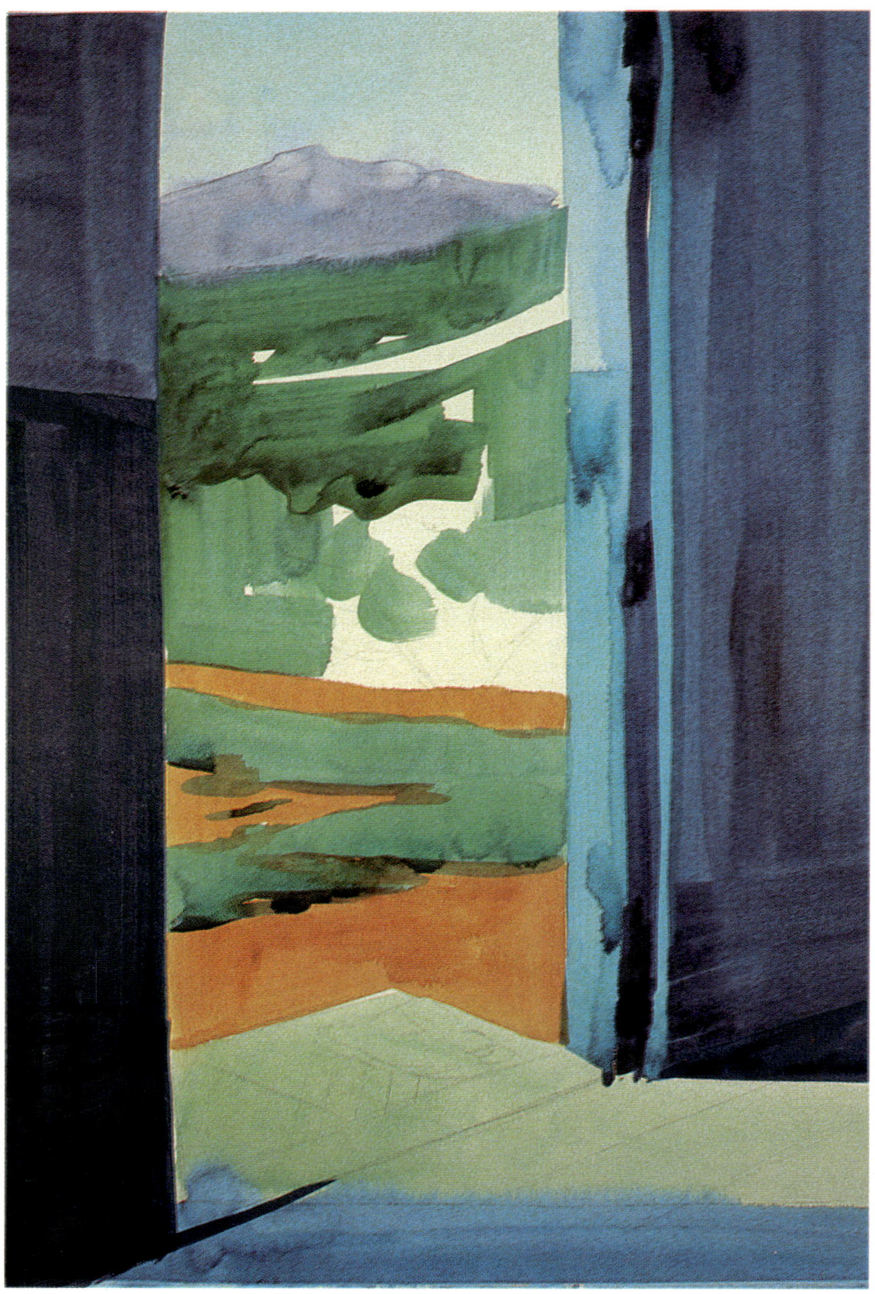

1 After sketching in the scene, I begin by washing in some vivid base colors, emphasizing the doorway as a frame for the landscape. I don't pay attention to detail at this point; I'm just trying to get a sense of the basic color scheme. Using a medium flat brush, I wash in the doorway with a mixture of phthalo blue and acra violet. Then I lay in a warm mix of white, cadmium yellow light, and a touch of brilliant blue for the floor.

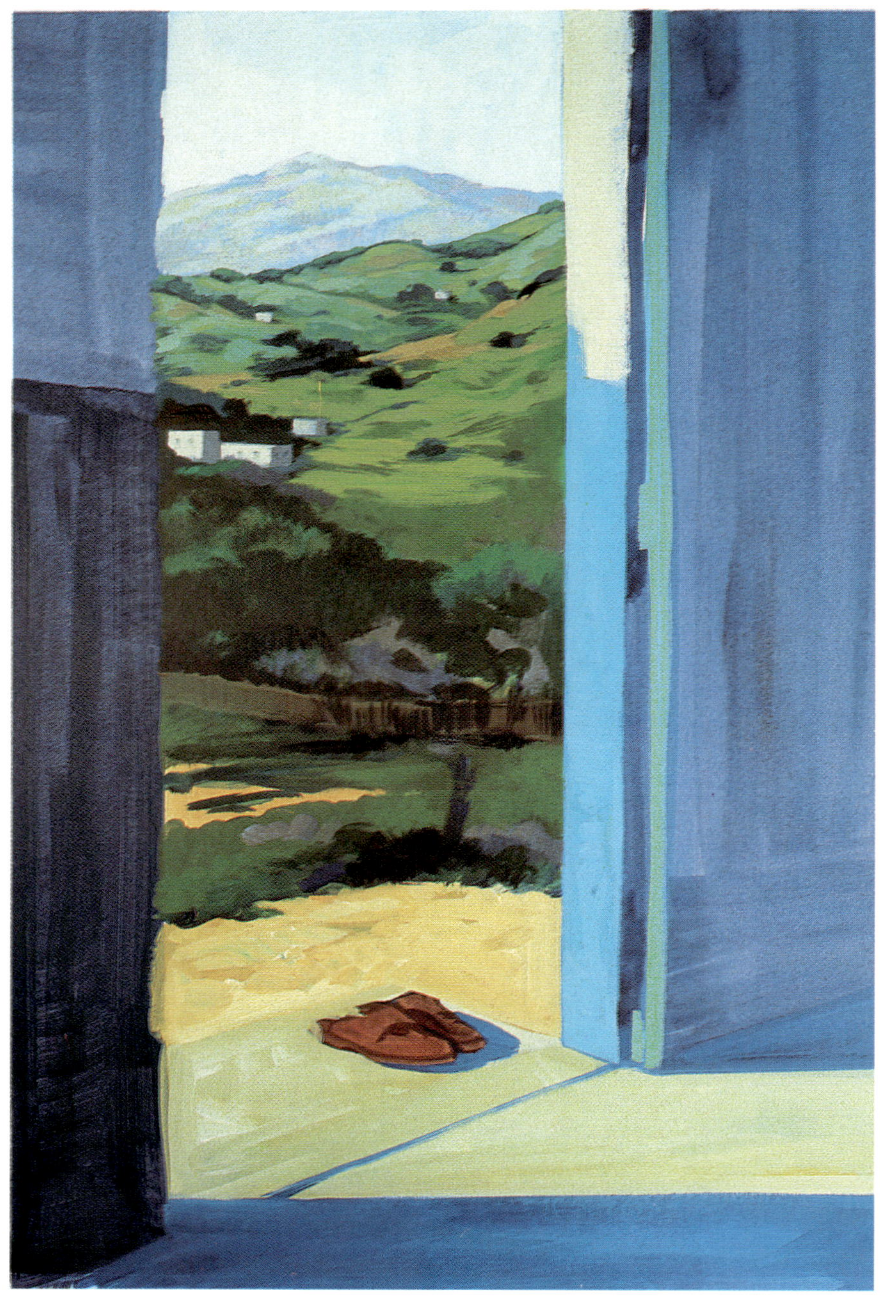

2 Next I begin to work opaquely, using thicker paint and starting with the background. As I move forward, I add sharper details and use a progressively brighter palette. Once my distant grounds are established, I work out the middle ground by painting in the stick fence, the gardens, and the fruit tree. I save my purest colors for the immediate foreground—the slippers and door.

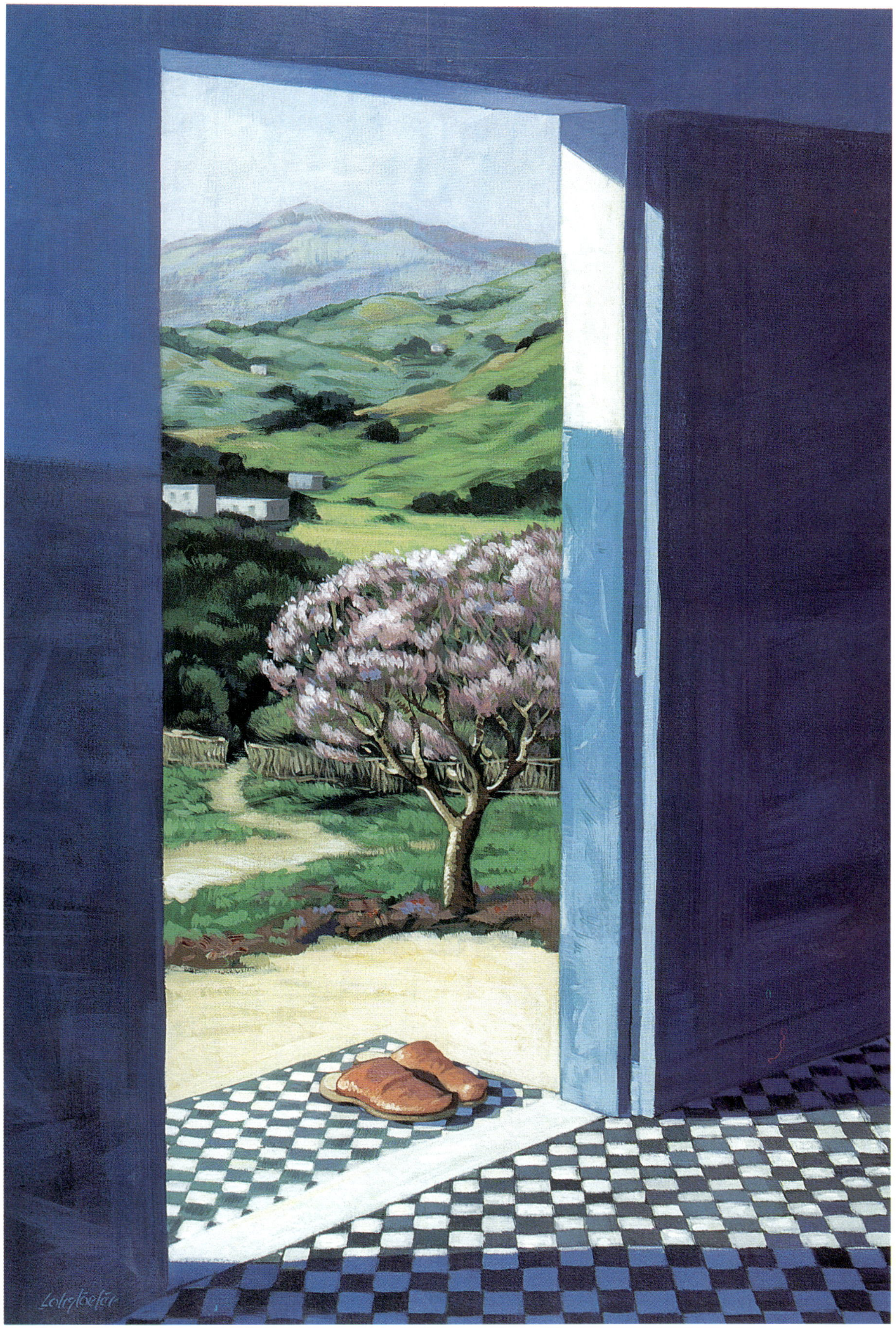

3 For the final details, I need to add bright touches of sunlight. I add white with a touch of cadmium red and cadmium yellow light to the outer edges of the fruit tree. I enhance the tile pattern with white highlights on the white squares and use brighter blues where the sun hits the doorway. Notice that there are many different blues in the tile—they lean toward green in the sun and are more purple in the shade. I use a small flat brush to add either turquoise green or acra violet as I shift from warm to cool tiles.

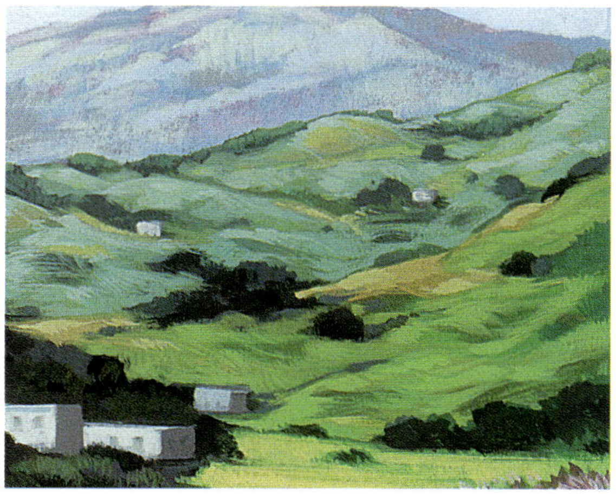

▲ **DISTANT HILLS** In the process of painting the middle ground, I've worked in a few stucco hillside homes. To help create a sense of depth, I gradually decrease the houses in size as they fade into the distance. When I paint the shadows, I think about my light source and the time of day; the late afternoon sun casts deep, cool shadows, so I add shadows to all the elements in the painting—even the tree trunk below has a sunny side and a shadowed side.

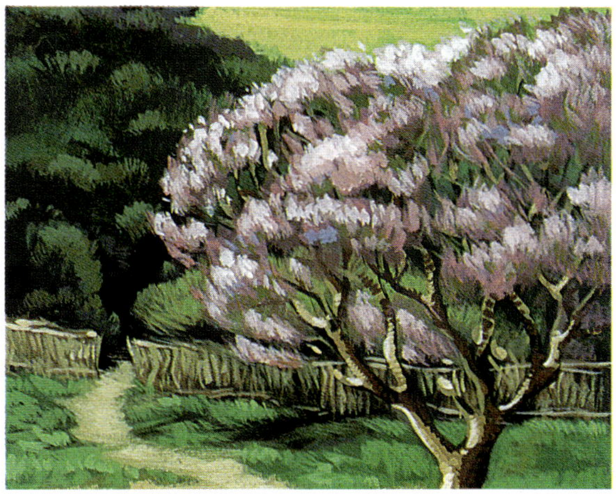

▲ **FRUIT TREE** Once I establish the green field, I add the tree trunk. By painting the tree in spring bloom, I bring it to the front of the middle ground. I use a small round brush to add details, creating small, irregular bunches of leaves and blossoms in greens and pinks. I use mixes of white, phthalo green, cadmium yellow light, and brilliant blue for the greens; then I add highlights with white, violet, cadmium red, phthalo green, and cadmium yellow light.

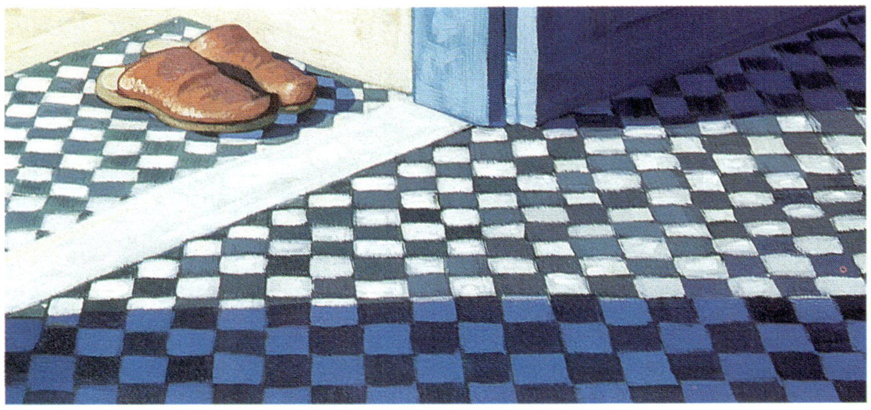

◄ **CHECKERED TILES** I use small flat brushes to block in the blue squares, letting the underpainting define the white squares. Then I drag a little of the blue over the underpainted white squares with a drybrush technique, so the tiles won't look as if they were cut out and pasted on the board.

Artist's Tip

When you have a complex pattern, like this tile floor, use a straightedge to sketch in the lines, or photocopy your reference photo and transfer it to your painting surface.

Simplifying Your Subject

I LOVE TO PAINT PATTERNED MATERIALS because they make such an interesting graphic impact. Since they have a sense of order that's both familiar and comforting, they immediately attract attention and draw the viewer into the picture. Although intricate patterns may seem to be complex, they're really quite simple to unravel and very fun to paint.

Paring It Down to the Essentials

Instead of trying to duplicate all the intricate details exactly, I simply paint my rough impression of the overall pattern; I look at it in terms of general shapes and masses of lights and darks. Although I like painting all sorts of patterns, from animal fur to woven rugs, I particularly like combining patterns in a painting, especially when they have contrasting designs and colors. My striped, orange cat and the geometric turquoise quilt he's lying on are a perfect example of such a contrast, and I'm sure you'll find many more such captivating examples when you start scouting out your own fascinating patterned subjects to paint.

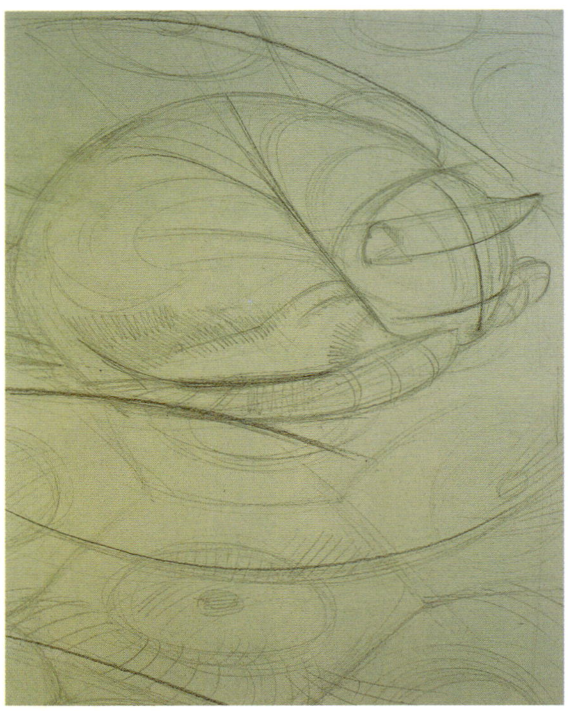

1 When I sketch out the composition on my support, I use simple circles to indicate the repeating pattern of the quilt, changing the angles slightly to show how the pattern curves around the folds of the fabric. To make the composition interesting, I raise the focal point—the cat—to the upper one-third of the composition. This also lets me show off a large portion of the quilt.

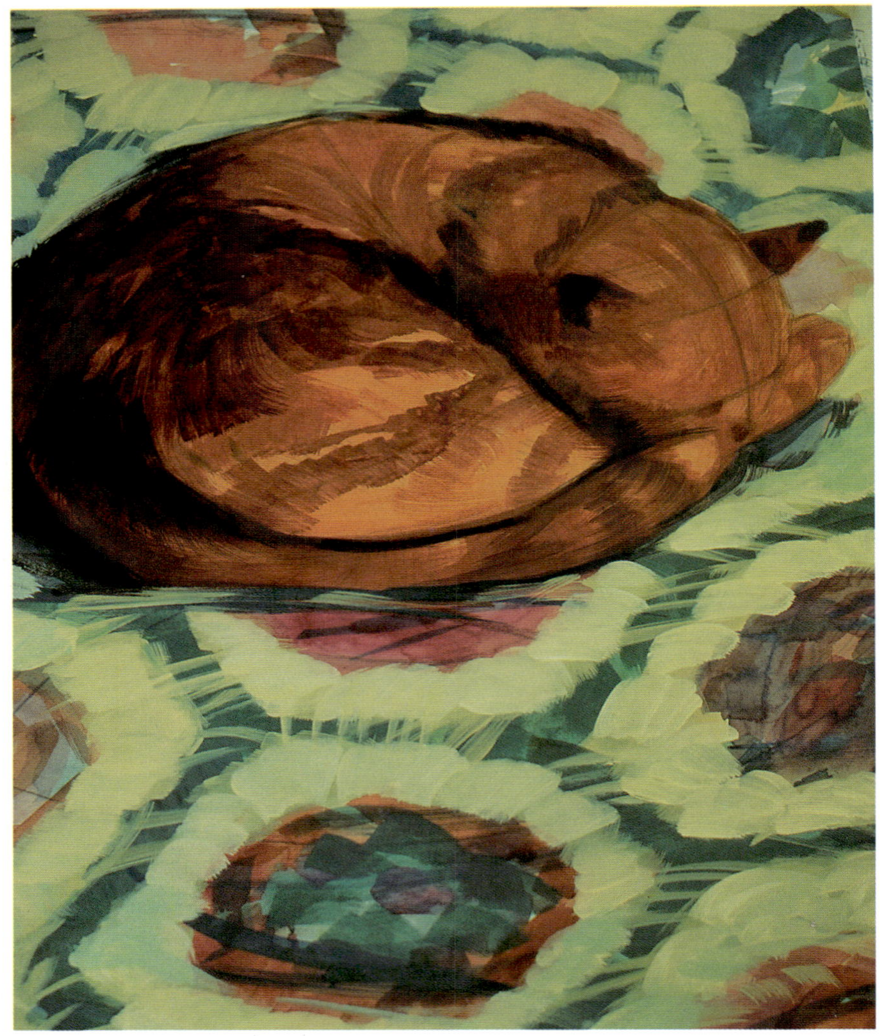

2 I lay in the underpainting with pure, rich color washes; then I reinforce my darkest values. I'm painting on a 30" x 40" canvas, so I use large brushes and work with bold, expressive strokes. I lay in all the different colors in the quilt; then I block in the cat with a mix of yellow ochre, cadmium orange, burnt sienna, and burnt umber.

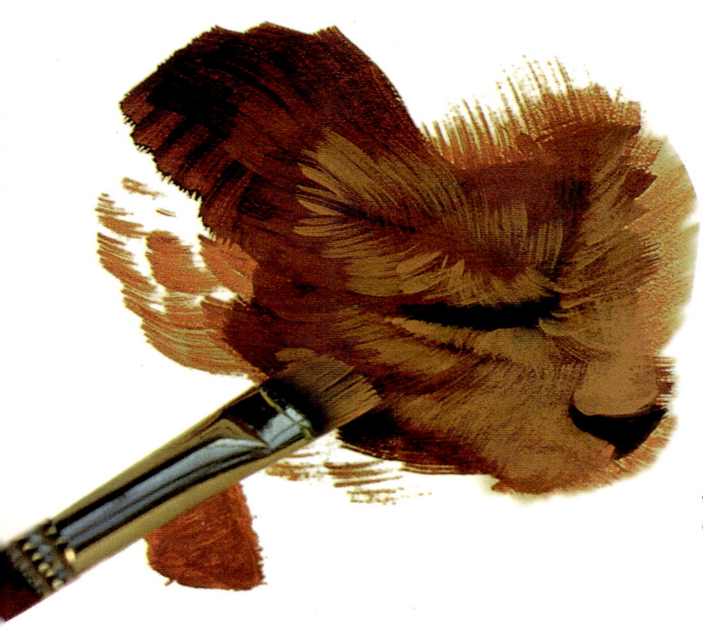

◄ **PAINTING FUR PATTERNS** I choose an old brush that has splayed bristles and load the dry brush with paint. As I stroke, I firmly press down the tip of the brush to spread apart the bristles even further. I drybrush layer after layer, working from the darker, purer colors up to the lighter, whitened values. These multiple layers of color give the fur realistic depth and dimension.

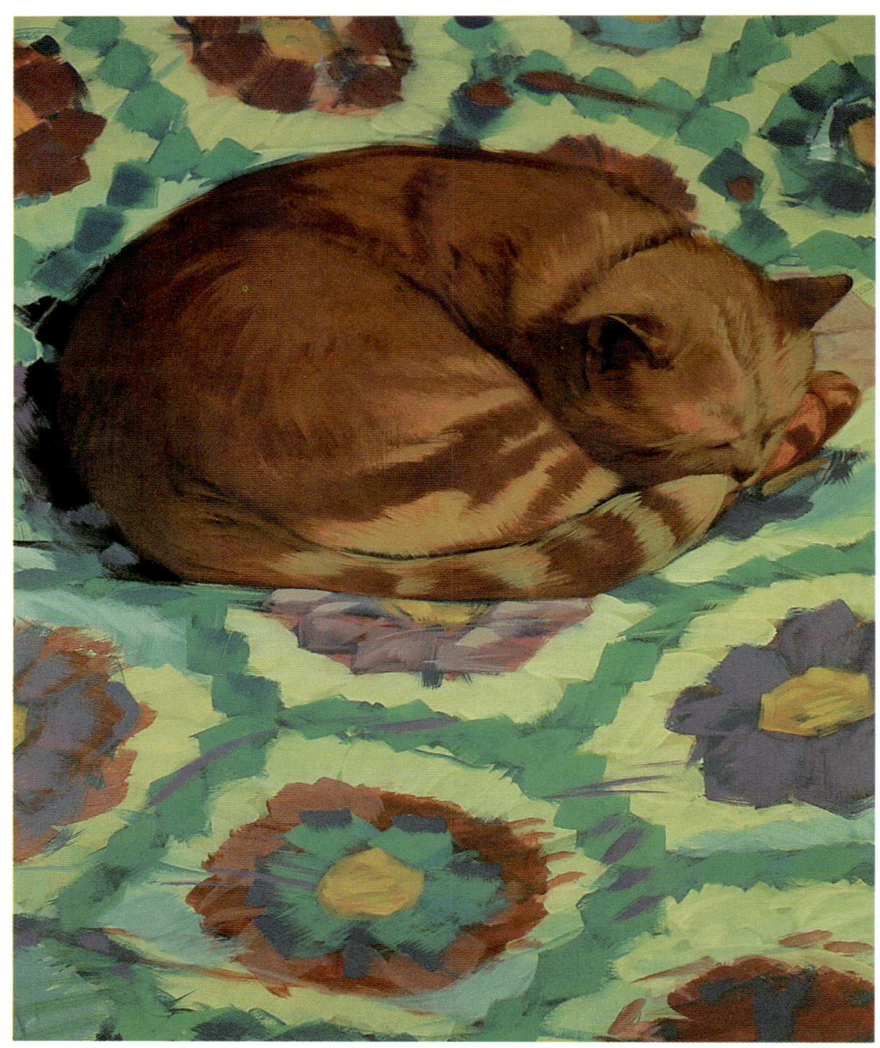

3 Working in a loose style with a medium flat brush, I paint from dark, saturated color to light, whiter values. I mix a warm turquoise, white, and a little cadmium yellow light for the green sections of the quilt pattern, using the edge of the brush where I want harder lines. Then I apply dots and dashes of color to merely suggest the details.

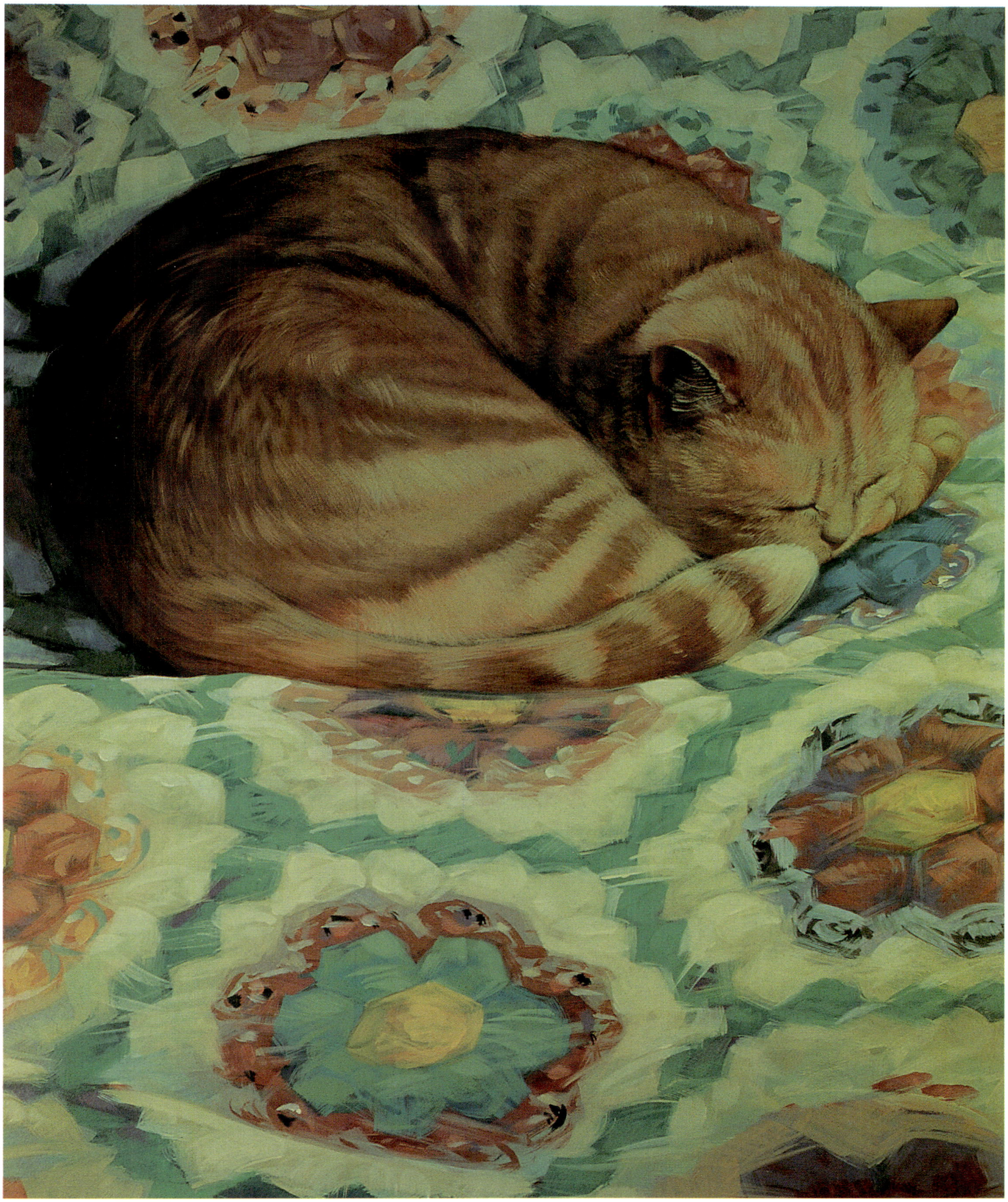

4 The light is shining in from a window at right, and even though it's a soft light, it's still an important element in the painting: Notice the way the light casts a shadow across the cat's back. Using the light source as a guide, I paint each fold of the quilt with a highlight and a shadow side; then I enhance the highlighted folds. To finish, I use a very small round brush to work in the highlights on the cat's face. Then I use the side of a stiff piece of paper to stroke in the fine lines of the cat's whiskers.

QUILT

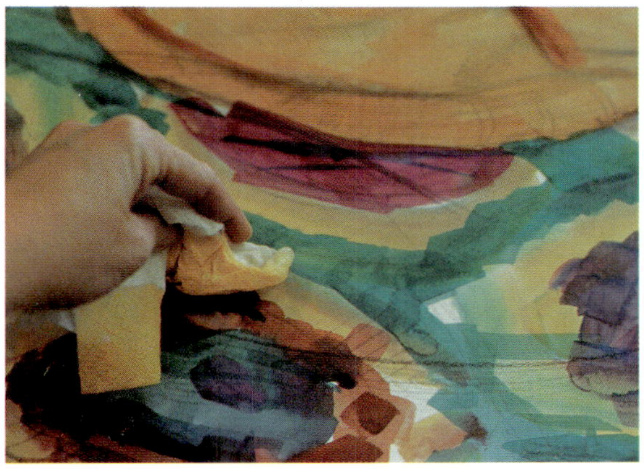

1 First I roughly block in the basic colors of the pattern on the quilt. Here I use a paper towel to quickly apply bold color, not worrying about precision or edges.

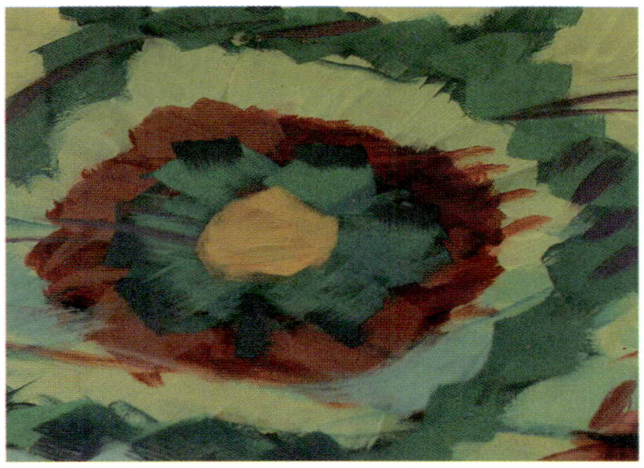

2 With a flat brush I begin building up the colors and defining the patterns, working from dark to light. I also suggest a few details, but I don't get too intricate yet.

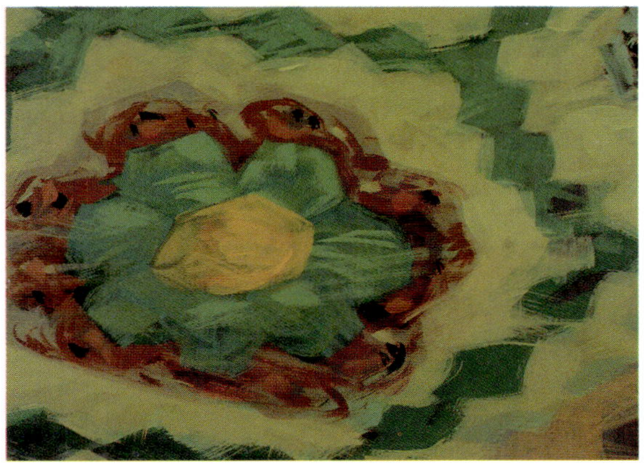

3 As I apply the lightest values, I add more detail, but I still don't try to duplicate all the intricate elements of the pattern. This simplified version works beautifully.

Focusing on Flowers

FLORAL STILL LIFES OFFER A WONDERFUL opportunity to learn and practice basic painting skills. I can test out a variety of color combinations, apply different textures, experiment with new strokes, and practice setting up appealing compositions. I can establish my own lighting conditions. And because acrylic dries so quickly, I don't have to wonder whether my flower subjects will wilt while I wait for a section to dry. I can easily finish an entire painting *alla prima*—all in one session!

Planning a Color Scheme

Planning your color palette before you begin to paint will save you time in the long run, and it will help make sure your painting is successful. Consider pushing the darker shadows of a piece and working mostly in medium and dark values—this can add a richer feel to your work. Try using a complementary palette to draw the eye into your painting as well. By placing the greens of the hydrangea and the vase next to the deep reds of the dahlia here, I've emphasized the vibrancy of the mid-tone reds. I've also kept the surrounding colors either complementary (green) or neutral so that the reds will be even more striking—the most vivid color on the canvas.

1 **In this piece, proportion is important. I'm working on a 36" x 48" canvas, and I want to make sure the vase, the flowers, and the backdrop all have the correct size relationships. Instead of drawing freehand on the canvas, where I risk losing sight of the whole composition, I sketch it out on paper first and then use a grid to transfer my sketch to the canvas (see the box at right).**

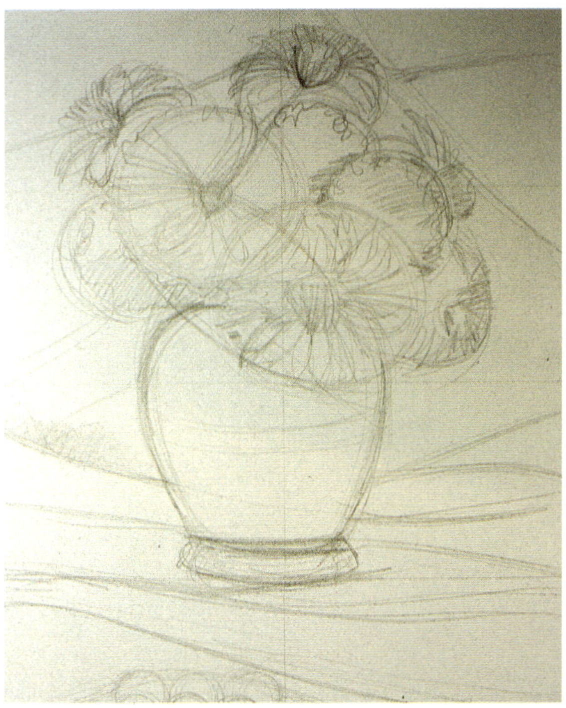

2 **I begin with saturated pure washes and a large bristle brush, splashing bold, deep tones across the canvas. I work in the hydrangea blossoms with deep purples, mossy greens, a blue-green, and spots of brown. I block in the main flowers with a combination of reds and suggest a few of the pattern elements in the drapery.**

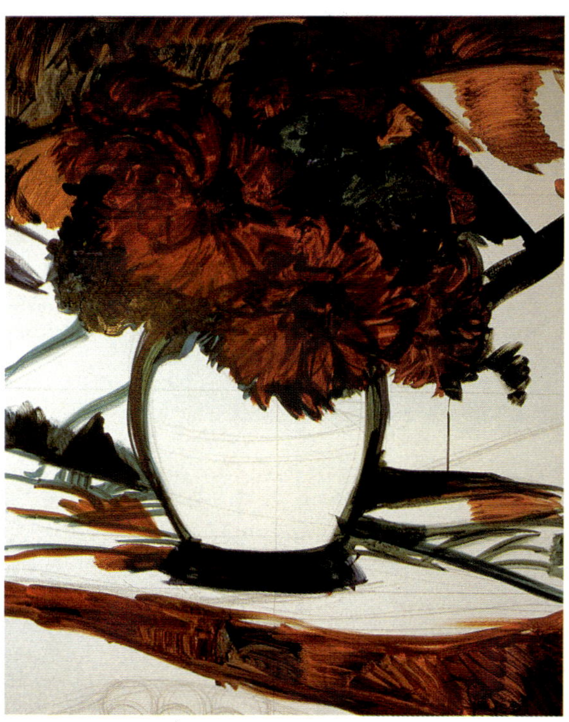

Using a Grid to Transfer Your Sketch

When I plan to paint on a large canvas, I often work out my composition on paper first with a smaller, simplified sketch. (I always make sure the paper has the same relative proportions as my canvas!) Then I translate the sketch to canvas using the grid method described below. Aside from the canvas, all I need is a t-square, a triangle or ruler, and a sketching tool.

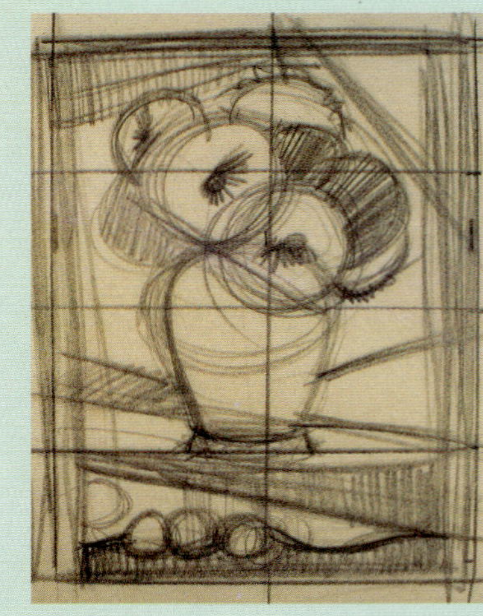

First I sketch out a simple drawing and check that all the proportions are correct. Then I divide the sketch into eighths and draw the same 8-square grid on the canvas.

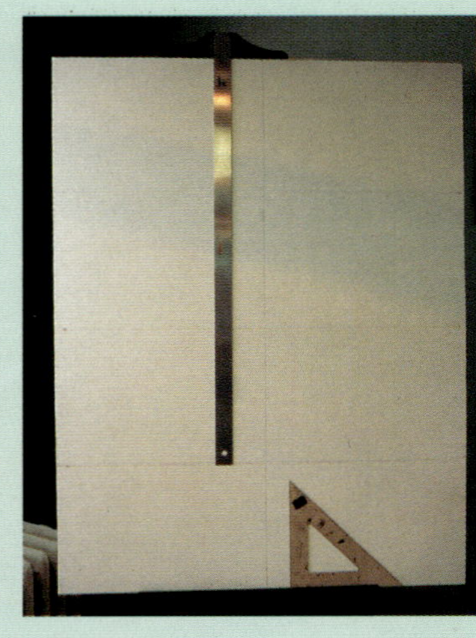

Using the sketch as a reference, I copy the lines in each square onto each corresponding square on my canvas. I draw one section at a time, instead of the whole composition at once.

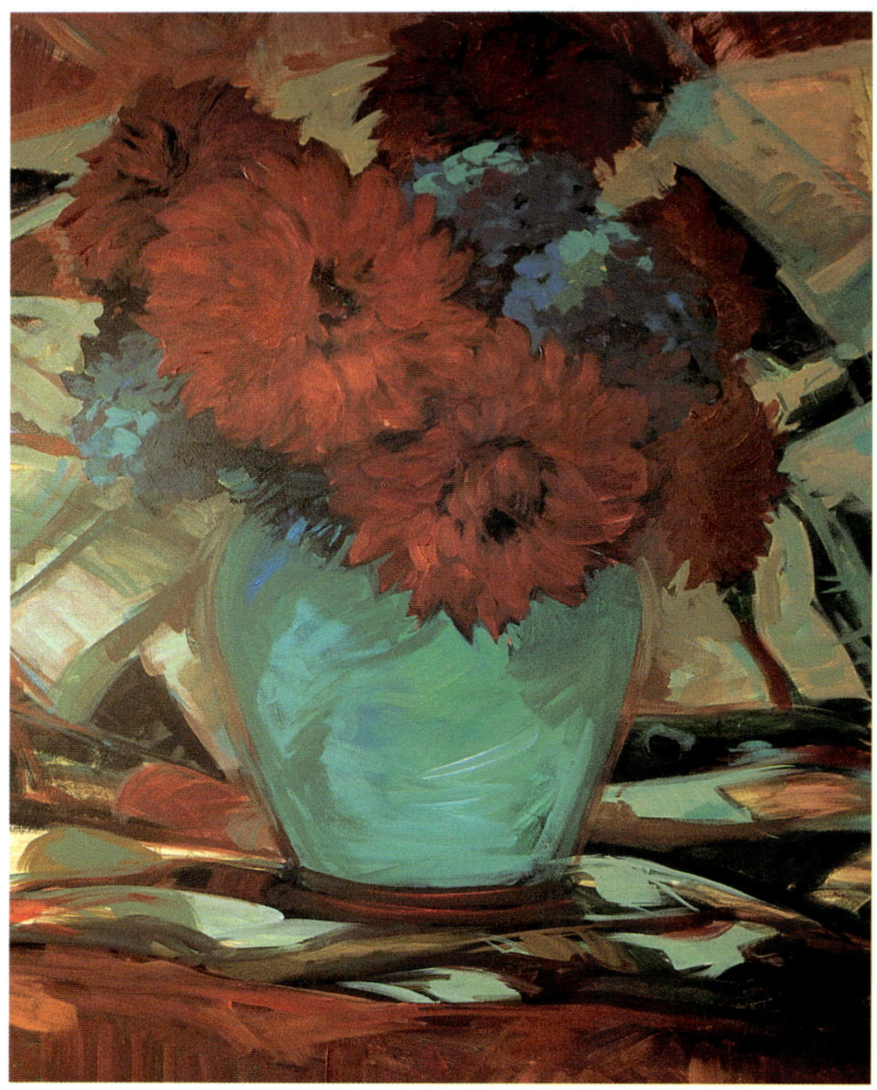

3 **I build up the dahlias with a mix of acra violet, naphthol crimson, and phthalo blue, plus white for opacity. Then I add spots of cadmium red and burnt sienna. I use a large bristle brush and mix turquoise green, phthalo blue, acra violet, white, cadmium orange, and yellow ochre for the vase, putting warm touches over my cool green underpainting.**

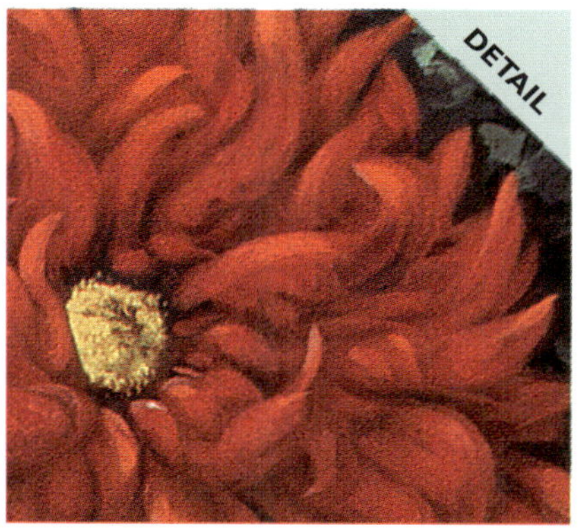

▲ **DAHLIA** For each petal, I use a large filbert and press down at the center, making a wide stroke. Then I lift up the brush to taper the stroke at the petal's point.

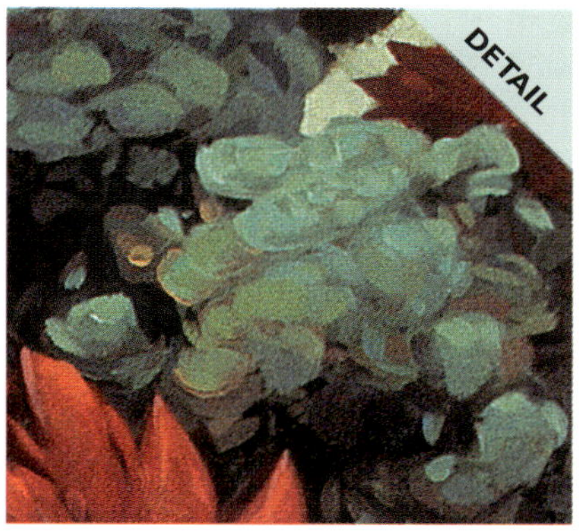

▲ **HYDRANGEAS** Because this flower has such a uniform pattern, I need to break it up a bit. I play with different brushes and brushstrokes to create a more natural, random petal pattern.

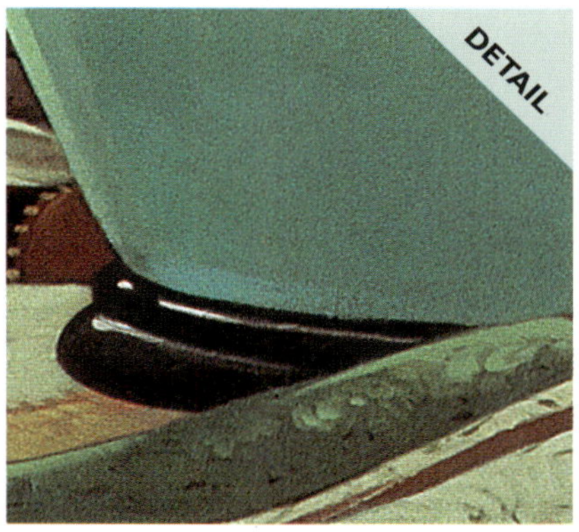

▲ **VASE** After scrubbing in the vase with a bristle brush, I switch to a small brush to highlight the gold centers of the flowers. Then I add highlights of pure white to the reflection on the vase and its black base.

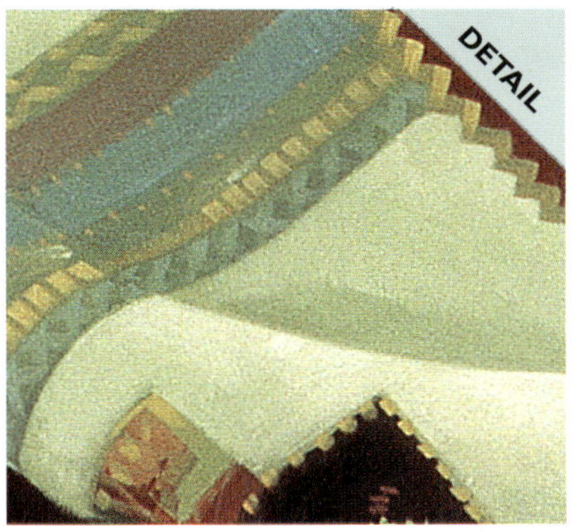

▲ **QUILT** This is a great exercise in painting abstract patterns. I tried to simplify the pattern as much as possible, creating large folds in the fabric and improvising my own designs where necessary.

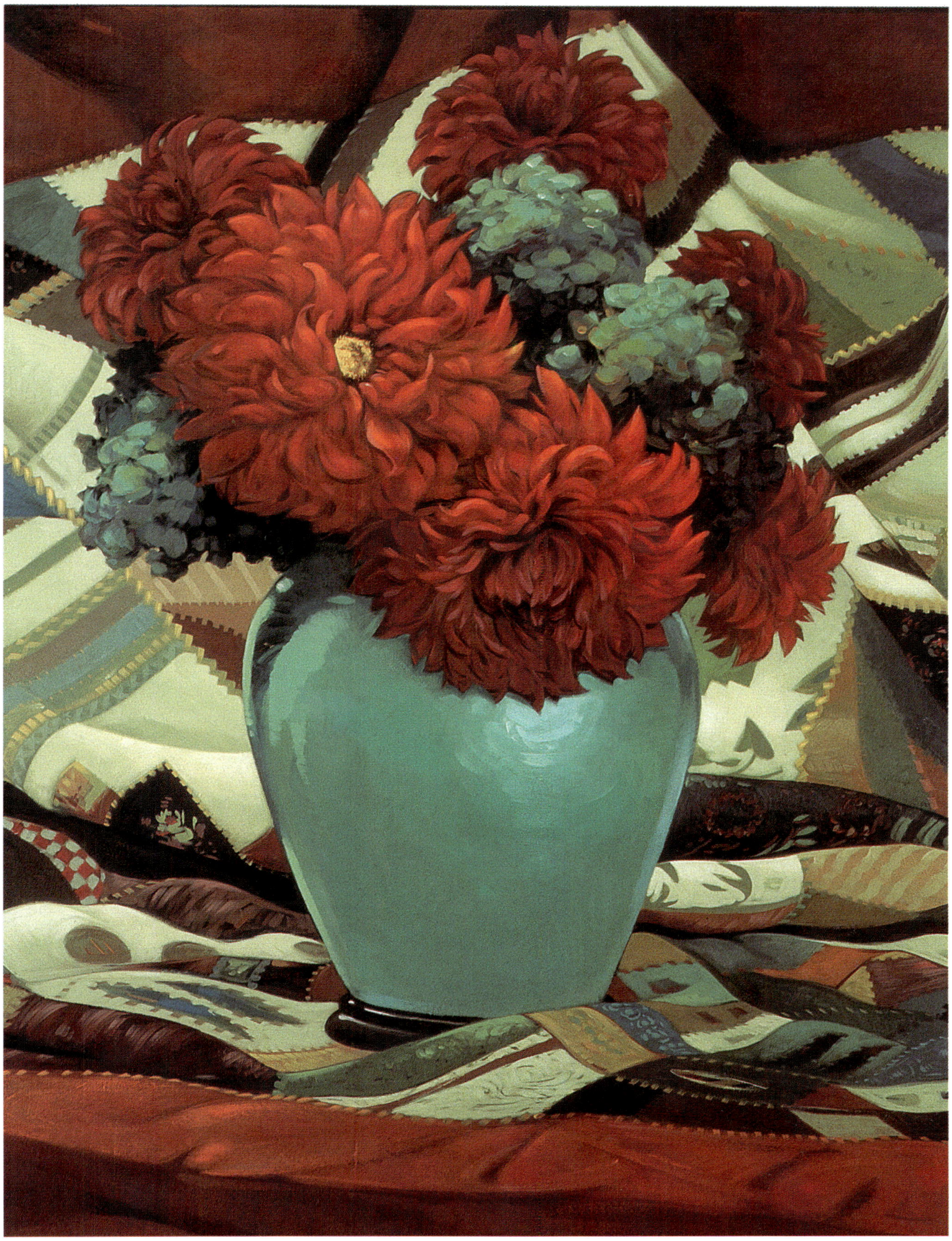

4 To keep the eye from being distracted, I put more detail in the foreground and less in the background. I use a small flat brush with a mix of yellow ochre, burnt sienna, and white to add the stitching details. Then I examine my quilt pattern and decide to add some lighter areas of white, burnt sienna, and turquoise green. Finally I punch up the red dahlia with bright highlights.

Wrapping It Up

Remember that you don't have to contrive complicated setups to make an interesting painting—there is just as much beauty in a simple grouping of flowers, like the one above, as there is in the finest works of the old masters. What makes your paintings lively is the creation of some visual excitement by making a dynamic composition, creating a mood with lighting, pairing complementary colors, or using a variety of different brushstrokes. And whatever you decide to paint, don't be afraid to experiment. Try something new. But above all else, enjoy yourself!

Artist's Tip

No two flowers are exactly alike. Practice drawing individual flowers to capture the personality of each one.

More Ways to Learn

Artist's Library

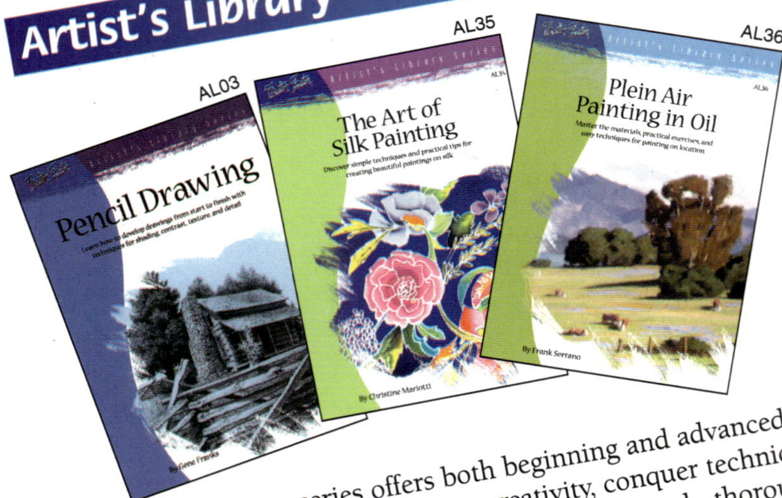

The **Artist's Library** series offers both beginning and advanced artists many opportunities to expand their creativity, conquer technical obstacles, and explore new media. You'll find in-depth, thorough information on each subject or art technique featured in the book. The books are written and illustrated by well-known artists who are qualified to help take eager learners to new levels of expertise.

Paperback, 64 pages, 6-1/2" x 9-1/2"

Collector's Series

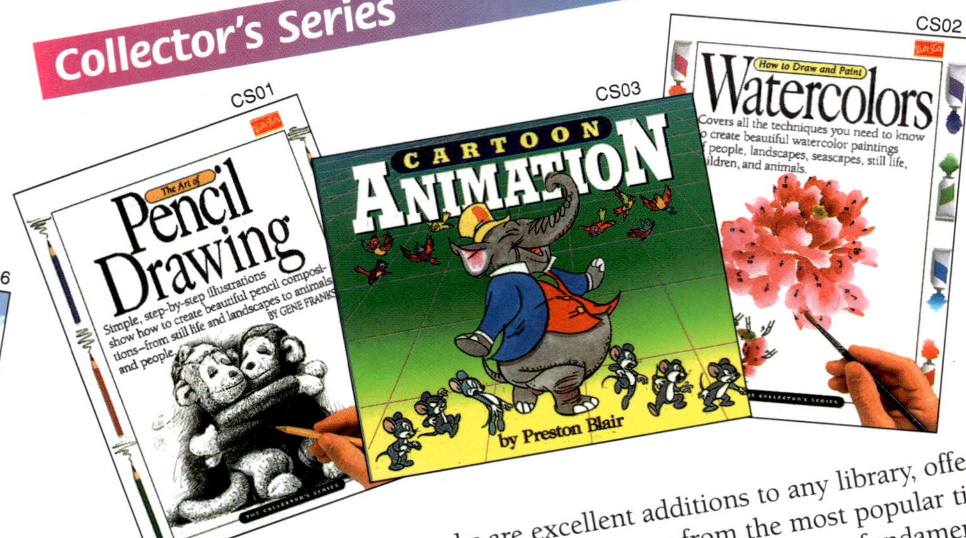

The **Collector's** series books are excellent additions to any library, offering a comprehensive selection of projects drawn from the most popular titles in our How to Draw and Paint series. These books take the fundamentals of a particular medium, then further explore the subjects, styles, and techniques of featured artists.

CS01, CS02, CS04: Paperback, 144 pages, 9" x 12"
CS03: Paperback, 224 pages, 10-1/4" x 9"

How to Draw and Paint

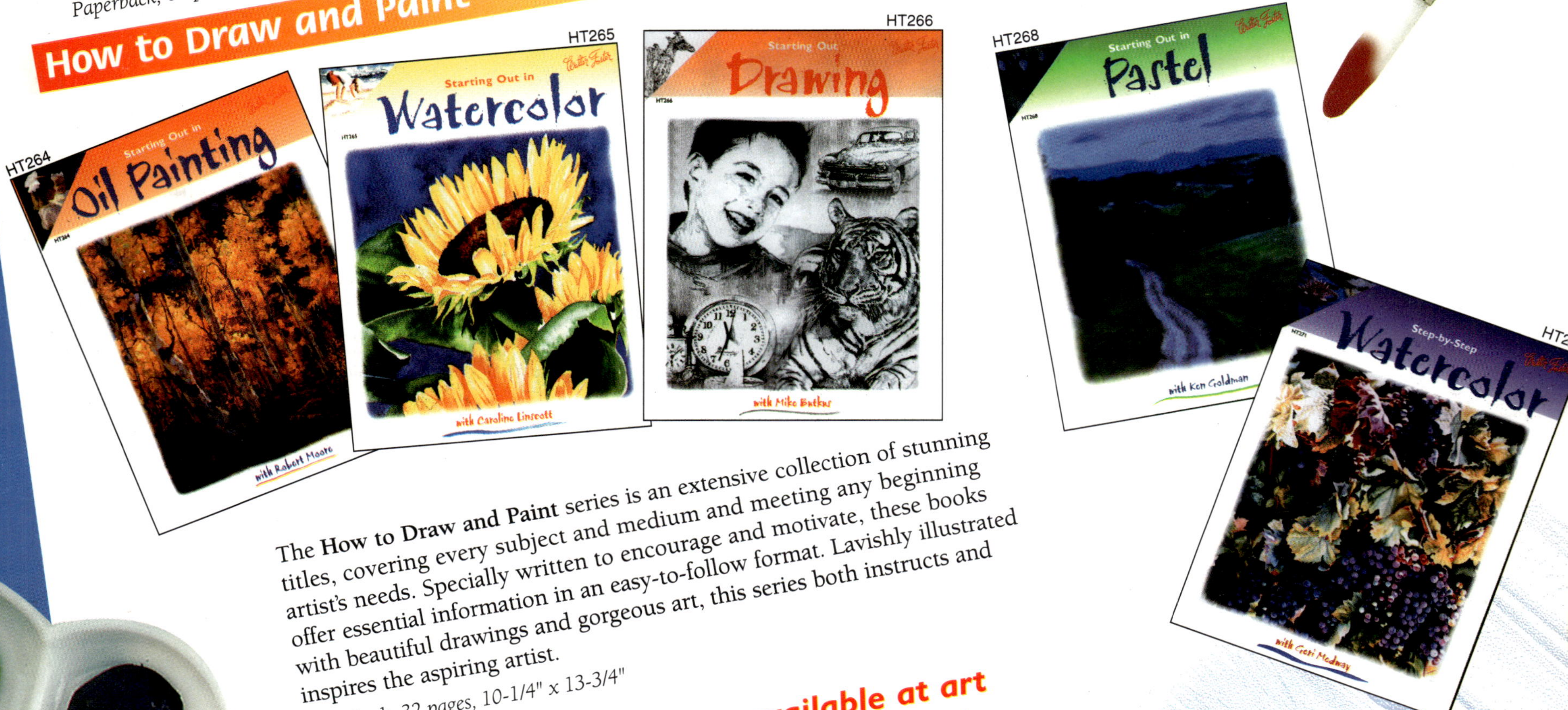

The **How to Draw and Paint** series is an extensive collection of stunning titles, covering every subject and medium and meeting any beginning artist's needs. Specially written to encourage and motivate, these books offer essential information in an easy-to-follow format. Lavishly illustrated with beautiful drawings and gorgeous art, this series both instructs and inspires the aspiring artist.

Paperback, 32 pages, 10-1/4" x 13-3/4"

Walter Foster products are available at art and craft stores everywhere. Write or call for a FREE catalog that includes all of Walter Foster's titles. Or visit our website at www.walterfoster.com

Walter Foster®

Walter Foster Publishing, Inc. • 23062 La Cadena Drive • Laguna Hills, CA 92653 • (800) 426-0099